D0563697

JOSEPH
God's Man in Egypt

Leslie B. Flynn

While this book is designed for the reader's personal enjoyment and profit, it is also intended for group study. A Leader's Guide with Victor Multiuse Transparency Masters is available from your local bookstore or from the publisher at $2.50.

VICTOR BOOKS

a division of SP Publications, Inc., Wheaton, Illinois

Offices also in Fullerton, California • Whitby, Ontario, Canada • London, England

Unless otherwise noted, Scripture quotations are taken from the King James Version.

Recommended Dewey Decimal Classification: 221.924
Suggested subject headings: JOSEPH; CHRISTIAN BIOGRAPHY; PROVIDENCE AND GOVERNMENT OF GOD

Library of Congress Catalog Number: 79-64820
ISBN: 0-88207-788-0

VICTOR BOOKS
a division of SP Publications, Inc.
P.O. Box 1825, Wheaton, Illinois 60187

CONTENTS

To Our Staff
Hank Beukema
David E. Hanson
Bryan Wilkerson
Donald O. Robertson
Mrs. Sandra Caselli
Mrs. Ruth Pedersen

Foreword

King Tut's Treasures attracted several million visitors in its recent six-city exhibit across the U.S.A.

The life of another Egyptian ruler, who lived three and a half centuries before King Tut, offers treasures of a different sort. The emotion-packed story of Joseph, suddenly elevated from prison to second-in-command of all Egypt, where he saved literally millions from starvation, is among the loveliest, best told, and most familiar episodes of scriptures.

Joseph has left us a legacy of inestimable spiritual worth. He faced many of the same problems confronting us today. From the example of this dreamer who became a doer we may learn how:

—To overcome envy
—To face adversity
—To resist illicit sexual advances
—To plan for the future
—To forgive those who wrong us

—To dispell doubts about forgiveness
—To have faith in God's promises
—To recognize the sovereignty of God, even in the wrongs done us by others.

Many historians place Joseph in the Hyksos period of Egyptian history, called The Second Intermediate Age (1780–1546 B.C.). The Hyksos were shepherd kings of Canaanite origin who took advantage of Egypt's internal strife to conquer the weakened nation. The sudden rise of a Semitic outsider to a place of leadership would understandably fit this era of Egyptian history. (See William S. Lasor, *Great Personalities of the Old Testament*, Old Tappan, New Jersey: Fleming H. Revell, 1959, pp. 43–45).

Joseph occupies as much space in the Book of Genesis as any other character, including Abraham. He is the link between Genesis and Exodus. His story explains how a handful of people left Canaan and became a numerous and settled Colony in Egypt. Understanding Exodus would be difficult without knowing about Joseph.

Besides his vital link in the historical chain, Joseph is probably the fullest type of Christ in the Old Testament, even though he is never mentioned as an antitype in the New Testament. Theologian Arthur W. Pink devotes 68 pages in his *Gleanings in Genesis* to list a literal 101 ways in which Joseph typifies Christ. Like Christ, for example, Joseph was specially loved by his father, hated and persecuted by his brothers, and finally exalted to a position where he became their savior. This study will not emphasize the typology of Joseph, however, but will handle it incidentally to the main practical lessons.

6

With few flaws in his character, Joseph may well be the most attractive figure in the Bible apart from Christ. Patient under persecution, resistant to temptation, magnanimous in forgiveness, he mirrors in so many ways the beauties of our "Fairest Lord Jesus."

Joseph's story not only interests children, but his example supports those bearing the brunt of adulthood's battles. His care for his aged father, as well as his own dying request, encourages those in the sunset of life. All ages may profit from the narrative's multifaceted lessons.

APPROXIMATE CHRONOLOGY OF JOSEPH

(ALL REFERENCES FROM GENESIS)

AT AGE

  0—BORN AT HARAN (30:22-24)

  7—HIS FATHER, JACOB, LEAVES HARAN (AND LABAN) AND IS REUNITED WITH ESAU, LIKELY A DIM MEMORY TO JOSEPH (3L-33)

12—HIS BROTHERS SLAY SHECHEMITES (34)

12—HIS MOTHER, RACHEL, DIES IN GIVING BIRTH TO BENJAMIN NEAR BETHLEHEM (35:16-20)

13—MEETS HIS GRANDFATHER, ISAAC; SETTLES IN SAME AREA (HEBRON) (35:27-29)

17—GIVEN COAT OF MANY COLORS (37:3)

17—DREAMS OF SHEAVES AND STARS BOWING TO HIM (37:5-11)

17—SOLD BY BROTHERS TO ISHMAELITES AND BOUGHT BY POTIPHAR (37:18-36)

22—MADE OVERSEER OF POTIPHAR'S HOUSE (39:1-6)

27—TEMPTED BY POTIPHAR'S WIFE, FALSELY ACCUSED, CAST INTO THE KING'S PRISON (39:7-23)

28—INTERPRETS DREAMS OF BUTLER AND BAKER, THEN FORGOTTEN BY BUTLER FOR TWO YEARS (40)

30—ELEVATED TO BE SECOND RULER OF EGYPT (41:1-44)

37—SEVEN YEARS OF PLENTY COME TO END, DURING WHICH JOSEPH STORES GRAIN (41:45-57)

39—HIS BROTHERS MAKE FIRST VISIT TO EGYPT. SIMEON HELD AS HOSTAGE (42)

39—SECOND VISIT BY BROTHERS; BENJAMIN FALSELY CHARGED (43:44)

39—JOSEPH REVEALS HIMSELF TO HIS BROTHERS, URGING THEM TO BRING ENTIRE FAMILY, ESPECIALLY JACOB, TO EGYPT (45)

40—JACOB, HIS SONS AND THEIR FAMILIES (ABOUT 70) VISIT JOSEPH AND MOVE TO EGYPT (46)

44—FAMINE ENDS (SEVEN YEARS OF PLENTY AND SEVEN YEARS OF FAMINE)

56—JOSEPH VISITS JACOB WHO BLESSES HIS (JOSEPH'S) TWO SONS (48)

56—JACOB BLESSES ALL HIS SONS, DIES AND IS BURIED IN CANAAN (49, 50:1-14)

57—THE BROTHERS DOUBT JOSEPH'S EARLIER FORGIVENESS (50:15-21)

110—JOSEPH DIES, IS EMBALMED AND PUT IN A COFFIN IN EGYPT (50:22-26)

1

Dark Threads—
Beautiful Pattern
Genesis 37—50

A bombing during the Korean War left a child named Kim blind, and forced her family to wander from place to place to beg for food. Her distraught father sold the eldest of his three daughters to a family to do housework. Then one day, in desperation, he threw his other two girls into a river. The younger drowned, but six-year-old Kim survived. For some reason, was able to float a bit, though she swallowed a lot of water and hit a rock. She was finally rescued by her own father. A few weeks later he left her at the door of a World Vision home that cared for the deaf and blind.

Four years later Kim came to the U.S. to be adopted by an American family. Here her lovely voice was discovered. She received a Fulbright scholarship with study in Vienna, Austria, and, later, invitations to sing in churches all over America. Today Kim Wickes serves on the Billy Graham team, singing at his crusades and over his TV programs.

Kim was reunited with her father during a visit to Korea in 1974. The Korean *Times* told the story of how this 27-year-old blind vocalist met her real father after 21 years.

Would all these good things have happened had Kim not suffered blindness and desertion?

Though the story of Joseph teaches many lessons, the theme that unites them all is the sovereignty of an all-wise God overruling the sordidness of man to work out His beautiful purpose. The episode as a whole shows how God can make the wrath of men to praise Him.

God wanted to preserve His people through a severe famine, so long before the famine occurred He transplanted one of their number to the land of plenty where he became the chief dispenser of grain. But to accomplish this, God used the mistreatment by others to move Joseph to Egypt and to elevate him to his position of influence.

As a minority and a nomadic group of only 70 in the midst of large, unfriendly, and well-established tribes, the family of Israel had dim prospects of growing into the innumerable progeny God had promised Abraham 200 years earlier (Gen. 12:1-3; 13:16). So the Lord transported the group to roomy, fertile, secluded Goshen where He sheltered it under the protection of the second-in-command of all Egypt. There, during the next two centuries, away from the corrupting influence of the Canaanites, the Israelites' number increased unhindered to about two million. But this growth stemmed indirectly from the terrible events in Joseph's life.

The story of Joseph has been called the Old Testament Romans 8:28 ("All things work together for good to them that love God"). Cruelty, slander, ingratitude—these tangled, dark threads were woven by a sovereign Artist into a beautiful, bright pattern. With God, there is no accident or chance. Man proposes; God disposes. Though others may mb treat us nastily, God is still on the throne, directing human affairs, able to use even dirty deeds against us to effect His perfect will.

The Thread of Cruelty

When Joseph's brothers saw that their father loved Joseph more than he loved any of them, and expressed his favoritism openly by making the lad a coat of many colors, "they hated Joseph, and could not speak peaceably unto him" (37:3-4).

When Joseph unabashedly told them of his two dreams foretelling his dominion over them, his brothers "hated him yet the more" (vv. 5-8).

One day when the 10 brothers had been gone several days tending their flocks, father Jacob sent Joseph to see how they were doing. After a three-day journey from the Hebron homestead to Shechem, some 50 miles to the north, Joseph learned that his brothers had moved to Dothan, 12 miles beyond. The brothers, spotting him afar off, "conspired against him to slay him," sneeringly calling him a "dreamer" (vv. 18-19). They spoke of tossing his corpse into a pit, then giving out the story that "some evil beast hath devoured him" (v. 20). But eldest brother Reuben, intending to rescue Joseph, suggested they put him in a dry well (vv. 21-22).

When Joseph reached his brothers they seized him,

stripped him of his special coat, and shoved him into a pit—Reuben was absent for some reason. Sitting down to eat, they ignored the cries of Joseph.

A caravan of Ishmaelites, carrying spices to Egypt, gave Judah the idea of selling Joseph to the merchants. "What profit is it if we slay our brother, and conceal his blood?" he asked. The brothers agreed, bargaining with the merchants for the price of 20 pieces of silver (37:26-28).

When Reuben discovered that his plan to rescue Joseph had been thwarted, he tore his clothes. Now they would have to concoct some story to explain the lad's disappearance. So they killed a goat, dipped Joseph's special coat in its blood, then brought it to their father, saying, "This have we found: know now whether it be thy son's coat or no?" Recognizing the coat, Jacob lamented, "An evil beast hath devoured him; Joseph is without doubt rent in pieces" (vv. 32-33). Heartbroken, he refused to be comforted (vv. 34-35).

What dark threads in Joseph's young life! Such bitter hatred issuing in envy, cruelty, deception, and slavery! But God was working. Who kept the brothers from killing Joseph? Who sent the caravan along just then? What kept Reuben from returning in time to rescue the lad and restore him to his father? God was weaving these dark threads into a beautiful pattern. The brothers thought they were making Joseph's dream of domination forever impossible. Instead, their very act of selling him into slavery was the first step toward Joseph's exaltation and the ultimate fulfillment of his dreams.

In fact, years later when Joseph revealed his identity to his terrified brothers, he told them that God had overruled their wickedness. "Now therefore be not grieved, nor angry with yourselves, that ye sold me hither; for God did send me before you to preserve . . . you a posterity in the earth, and to save your lives by a great deliverance. So now it was not you that sent me hither, but God" (45:5-8).

Joseph wasn't denying their sin or lessening their guilt. But sensing the sincerity of their repentance, he wished to minimize their pain by pointing out how God used the combination of cruelty, chicanery, and captivity to work out His perfect will.

The Thread of Slander

Joseph was carried by the Ishmaelites (also called Midianites in 37:28), down to Egypt, perhaps bound to a bale of merchandise loaded on a camel's back. The merchants, arriving in Egypt, sold Joseph to Potiphar, an officer of Pharaoh and captain of his guard (39:1).

The lot of a slave in Egpt was usually hopeless. Historians tell us that engineering feats such as the pyramids could have been accomplished only by the use of slaves whose lives were regarded as cheap and therefore easily disposable.

Was it chance that deposited Joseph in an upper-class home with close links to Pharaoh? Was it chance that gave Joseph favor in the sight of his master so that Potiphar made him overseer of his household affairs?

Joseph's handsome appearance did not go unnoticed by Potiphar's wife. When she repeatedly tried to seduce him, he firmly spurned her advances. One day, however, when he was alone in the house on business, he was again propositioned by Mrs. Potiphar, who grabbed him by his cloak. When he fled, she held onto the garment and used it as "evidence" of attempted rape by her husband's most trusted slave. Angry Potiphar ordered Joseph placed in the king's prison (39:17-20).

Perhaps Mrs. Potiphar thought she had gotten rid of Joseph when he was incarcerated. But in reality, her frame-up only advanced the train of events which led to Joseph's elevation to second-in-command of Egypt. To Joseph, the loss of his master's favor by such slander and the resulting imprisonment must have meant additional dark threads. But some day he would see how they were woven into a bright, beautiful pattern.

The Thread of Ingratitude

In prison Joseph prospered under the goodness of the Lord, so that the warden placed everything under Joseph's jurisdiction (39:21-23). Eventually two of Pharaoh's officers, a baker and a butler, were imprisoned and placed under Joseph's charge.

One morning Joseph, noting their sad faces, learned of their dreams the night before, which they could not interpret. Through the wisdom of God Joseph told the butler that in three days he would be restored to his position, and informed the baker that in three days he would be hanged. Joseph begged the butler to put in a good word to Pharaoh on his return to office, asserting his innocence of the charges for which he was in jail (40:14-15).

Joseph's request for the butler's help did not evidence lack of faith. God's sovereignty doesn't rule out man's responsibility. Joseph became a co-worker with the providence of God—his efforts fell in with God's plan.

Joseph's interpretations of the dreams proved true. Though the butler was restored, he proceeded to forget Joseph (v. 23). The butler's insensitivity seemed to weave another dark thread in Joseph's life, but his ingratitude really paved the way for Joseph's exaltation. Had the butler remembered Joseph immediately on his restoration to Pharaoh's favor, the most Joseph would have received would have been his freedom. But when two years later all the magicians and wise men of Egypt could not interpret Pharaoh's dreams, the butler's memory was suddenly refreshed. Joseph was summoned to Pharaoh's court, where he interpreted the ruler's dreams so sensibly that Pharaoh put Joseph in charge of all the grain. The butler's providential forgetfulness sparked the final link that catapulted Joseph from prison to second-in-command over all Egypt.

Years later Joseph's brothers came for grain. After testing them to make sure they were genuinely sorry for their previous cruel behavior, Joseph revealed himself to his brothers. Then he made arrangements for his father and family to move down to Egypt where they could survive the famine and multiply into a large nation.

What If . . .

A dreamer who slept one night by the caravan track which ran near Egypt dreamed he saw a crescent moon which shone on a group of tents beside the road. One tent was open, revealing several men and

one boy, whose youthful hands and feet were bound.
All the men were sleeping, but the captive lad was
biting through the ropes on his wrist and soon would
have freed himself. Just then one of the dogs in the
caravan began to yelp, causing a couple of men to stir.
Immediately the dreamer, sympathetic to the boy,
moved toward the dog, intending to strangle it before
it woke the man and prevented the lad's escape.

But an angel quietly appeared nearby, telling the
dreamer not to meddle. "If you stop the dog, the boy
will escape. Let me show you what will happen."
Then followed a quick view of history for several hundred years, as it would have been had the dreamer
killed the cur and allowed the boy to escape. For two
days and nights the boy ran till he reached the tent of
an old man who was holding a coat stained with goat
blood, which the man thought was his son's. The two
fell into each other's arms.

The dreamer was now more than satisfied that he
had let the lad escape. But the panorama kept moving. Next came burning drought with streams drying
up and fields yielding no crops. When the family of
that father and son began to scrape the bottom of their
provisions, the brothers started forth toward Egypt
where they were sure would be some grain. But when
they reached the border of Egypt, soldiers stood
guard to keep everyone out. No one in Egypt had
known of the coming famine. No one had advised the
storing of grain during the seven plenteous years. So
Egypt permitted no hungry mouths to cross its fron-
tiers. Weakly the brothers turned around for home.
With hope dashed, one by one they dropped beside
the road, none having the strength to bury the other.

Back home, the wives, the elderly, and the children, all perished. None of Jacob's family was left, no children of Israel.

The years sped by. Great empires came and went: Babylon, Media-Persia, Greece, and Rome, but no Judea nor Galilee ever existed. No Messiah was ever born. No shepherds. No wise men. No Calvary. No Resurrection. No Jesus. No New Testament.

The dreamer was sorry that in his dream he had strangled the dog. But the angel reminded him that he hadn't really choked the dog, but had been shown what would have been, had he done so. So, the dreamer did not strangle the dog that night, letting the boy continue his way as a slave to Egypt.

The Wisdom of God

The lone survivor of a shipwreck found himself on an uninhabited island. After a while he managed to build a hut where he placed some food he had gathered. Every day he scanned the horizon for any passing ship. One day he spotted a boat. He waved frantically. But the ship disappeared over the horizon. Sadly he returned to his hut, only to find it in flames. Next day a ship arrived—the same one that had passed the day before. The captain explained, "We saw your smoke signal."

What may seem like an accident unplanned by man may turn out to be an incident planned by God in His great design. A disappointment may really be His appointment.

Years ago a tornado struck the prairies of Minnesota, killing many, injuring hundreds, and almost demolishing the town of Rochester. An elderly doctor

and his two sons, just out of medical school, worked
for days aiding the stricken. Their heroic work did not
go unnoticed. Financial backing was offered to build a
hospital, provided the doctor and sons would take
charge. In 1889 they opened a clinic which soon attracted wide attention. Today people come from all
walks of life to the Mayo Brothers Clinic. Out of disaster came blessing. The poet William Cowper wrote:

> God moves in a mysterious way
> His wonders to perform,
> He plants His footsteps in the sea,
> And rides upon the storm.

When relating her sufferings in the Ravensbruck
concentration camp in World War II, Corrie ten
Boom often shows the reverse side of an embroidered
bookmark which seems to be nothing but a senseless
mass of tangled threads. Then she turns the bookmark
to the front, where the threads spell out in a beautiful
design, *God Is Love*. Then she quotes,

> My life is but a weaving
> Between my Lord and me;
> I cannot choose the colors
> He worketh steadily.
> Ofttimes He weaveth sorrow,
> And I in foolish pride
> Forget He sees the upper,
> And I, the under side.
>
> Not till the loom is silent
> And the shuttles cease to fly
> Shall God unroll the canvas
> And explain the reason why
> The dark threads are as needful

In the Weaver's skillful hand
As the threads of gold and silver
In the pattern he has planned.
                              — from Grant Colfax Tullar's
                              poem, "The Loom of Time"

When sometimes situations seem out of control, our vision should not focus on the wicked machinations of men, but rather on the overruling activity of God. The supreme illustration of God's wise sovereignty in bringing good out of evil is the crucifixion of Jesus. God overrode the wickedness of those who crucified Him, and who perpetrated the worst crime in all history, by using the cross as an instrument of salvation. Peter put it this way on the Day of Pentecost, "Him, being delivered by the determinate counsel and foreknowledge of God, ye have taken, and by wicked hands have crucified and slain, whom God hath raised up" (Acts 2:23-24).

This truth found its way into an early church prayer: "The kings of the earth stood up, and the rulers were gathered together against the Lord, and against His Christ . . . both Herod, and Pontius Pilate, with the Gentiles, and the people of Israel, were gathered together, 'For to do whatsoever Thy hand and Thy counsel determined before to be done'" (Acts 4:26-28).

About two decades after Joseph first revealed himself to his brothers with the comforting truth that God's providence had brought good out of the evil deed, Joseph had to reassure his brothers of this same truth. After their father's death, the brothers thought

Joseph would surely now seek revenge for their earlier cruelty. Joseph responded, "Ye thought evil
against me; but God meant it unto good, to bring to
pass, as it is this day, to save much people alive"
(50:20). Says the poet Richard Wilton,

> Heaven's favourite down a darksome pit
>   they cast,
> His rich-hued robe and lofty dreams
>   deriding;
> Then, from his tears their ruthless faces
>   hiding,
> Sell him to merchants, who with spicery
>   passed.
> The changeful years o'er that fair slave fled
>   fast,
> Behold him now in glorious chariot riding,
> Arrayed in shining vestures, and presiding
> O'er Egypt's councils—owned by Heaven at
>   last.
> In pit or palace, God's own hand was
>   weaving
> The 'many-coloured' texture of his days,
> The brightest tints till last in wisdom
>   leaving.
> So when dismal paths our feet are sinking,
> Let us be looking soon for lightsome rays,
> For our wise Father 'thoughts of peace' is
>   thinking.

Spurgeon put it this way, "From threatening clouds
we get the refreshing showers; from our worst troubles come our best blessings. The bitter cold sweet-

ens the ground; the rough winds fasten the roots of the old oaks. Many times in our affliction we imagine that God's plan is ending in disaster, but actually He is only moving us on to circumstances that will bring new benefits now, and new rewards in eternity."

2

Watch Out for Envy
Genesis 37

When a man's new Cadillac developed a rattle in the front door on the driver's side, he took it back to the dealer, who tried in vain to remedy it. Finally the dealer took the door panel off. Inside was a bolt with this note tied to it, "Serves you right. You're too rich!"

Envy. It helped nail Christ to the cross. The Pharisees were riled at Jesus' superiority in word and deed. Pilate correctly diagnosed the cause of His arrest. He "knew that for envy they had delivered him" (Matt. 27:18).

The Brothers' Envy

Envy almost caused the murder of Joseph. The roots of his brothers' envy toward him were complex. they reached not only into his brothers' minds, but into his father's and his own as well.

His father's favoritism. Joseph was the son of Jacob's favorite wife, Rachel. For 12 years he was not only the only son of Rachel, but the youngest of all Jacob's sons. He undoubtedly received a lot of attention, for with his half-brothers grown, father Jacob had more time to enjoy the little lad. The record clearly states, "Israel loved Joseph more than all his children, because he was the son of his old age" (37:3).

Nothing is said of Joseph's early life. Born in Mesopotamia, he must have been six or seven years old when his father decided to leave the employ of Laban, his grandfather. Perhaps Joseph vaguely recalled the flight from Laban, and the tense meeting with Uncle Esau (Gen. 31—33). He probably remembered the wicked slaughter of the Shechemites by his 10 brothers (v. 34). Made motherless at 12, when Rachel died after giving birth to Benjamin, his only full brother, Joseph was probably thrown closer to his father (35:16-20).

The story begins with Joseph at about 17 years of age, when Jacob clearly established his favoritism by giving Joseph a special coat. Translated by the RSV as "a long robe with sleeves," the coat was not a many-colored patchwork, but rather an ankle-length tunic made of the finest material, decorated with an embroidered narrow stripe of color around the bottom of the skirt and sleeves. Young Joseph, parading idly around in his fancy robe, irked the brothers no end. The record says, "When his brethren saw that their father loved him more than all his brethren, they hated him, and could not speak peaceably unto him" (v. 4).

Though Joseph's brothers were justified in their resentment over their father's favoritism, it is never right to allow irritation to develop into hate and envy. They should have gone to Jacob and stated their feelings rather than let their root of bitterness defile the family relationships (Heb. 12:15). It is possible, however, that they thought protest useless, for in that patriarchal society, father was king.

Joseph's flaunting of his dreams. The brothers' envy was fanned into greater flame when Joseph related a dream in which their sheaves of grain bowed down to his sheaf. Their hatred of him piqued, they asked, "Shalt thou indeed reign over us?" Then Joseph unwisely proceeded to tell them a second dream in which sun, moon and 11 stars made obeisance to him (vv. 8-9).

Joseph couldn't help dreaming his dreams, of which the meaning was clear, but he could have refrained from relating them to his family. Either he was naive, or he was mildly arrogant. Even his doting father rebuked his favorite at this point, "What is this dream that thou has dreamed? Shall I and thy brethren indeed come to bow down ourselves to thee to the earth?" (v. 10)

The malice of the brothers. Though the father's favoritism and Joseph's braggadosio contributed to the envy of the brothers, they were responsible for letting this base passion develop into fiendish deeds.

Envy is among the darkest, seamiest, vilest, and most devilish of sins, a vice which by itself proves the depravity of man. Envy may be defined as ill will toward a person because of his superiority. Note the two elements: *ill will* and *superiority.*

A person superior in position and power may be the object of envy. Someone once said, "Uneasy lies the head that wears the crown." Satan aspired to God's throne. Two hundred and fifty princes were swallowed up by the ground because they envied Moses (Ps. 106:16). The Books of Kings and Chronicles relate a series of murders of kings by jealous usurpers.

Many a church member has chafed in envy because someone else was selected chairman of a committee, emcee for a banquet, deacon, elder, or soloist for an important occasion.

Superiority may be evidenced in possessions. The have-nots find it easy to be rough on the rich. A new dress, a new home, or a souped-up jalopy may spur envy. Affluent Isaac "had possession of flocks, and possession of herds, and great store of servants; and the Philistines envied him" (Gen. 26:14).

Joseph was a handsome young man (Gen. 39:6). When Farrah Fawcett Shampoo, named after the TV star, came on the market, it didn't sell. One of the reasons, said a store official, "Women are jealous of her."

Joseph also seemed superior in moral rectitude, as reflected in the "evil report" he brought back of his brothers' conduct. For this some accuse him of being a tattle-tale (37:2). On the other hand, if the brothers were guilty of some wrong which should have been reported to his father, silence would have shown cowardice or compliance in their evil. If so, he was not talebearing but doing his duty. His high moral code was later displayed in his resistance to Mrs. Potiphar's advances (39:9). Because darkness dislikes light, his brothers hated him.

Had Joseph not given evidence of some superior ability, he would have looked ridiculous in his special coat, making his brothers laugh instead of envy. Also, his brothers would have deemed his dreams ludicrous. But because he did exhibit superior qualities, the truth of his dreams hit home.

Envy is a backhanded compliment, a tacit admission of inferiority. You have to be little to belittle. Envy says, "I'm not up to you. You're a better soloist, a prettier woman, a more efficient committee member."

The idea of bowing to Joseph was intolerable to the brothers, making it easy for them to want to get rid of him. This leads to the second element in our definition of envy: *ill will* (at another's superiority). Malice is an essential component of envy. The person who says, "I envy you. I wish I had what you have, but I'm glad you have it," does not rightly use the word *envy*. Genuine envy involves ill will; the preceding remark expresses only good will.

Aroused by another's superiority, envy feels pain, grief, annoyance, displeasure, resentment, and or regret toward a person. Envy is that rankling when someone else gets praise or promotion. It is also that despicable twinge of delight when your neighbor's new car gets a dent in its fender.

Envy tarnishes one's speech, prompting censure, name-calling, unfounded criticism, and sinister insinuations. Someone has called it "higher criticism"— criticism of someone higher.

Envy can manifest itself in horrendous deeds. When Joseph's brothers spotted their father's pet coming in his special coat, and recalled his vaunt of domination, they said one to another, "Behold, this dreamer cometh. Come now therefore, and let us slay him, and cast him into some pit, and we will say, Some evil beast hath devoured him and we shall see what will become of his dreams" (37:19-20).

Results of Envy

Envy tends to run more easily between persons in the same line of work. The theological professor is not envious of the professional wrestler. Nor does the musician envy the football player. Rather, doctor is more likely to envy doctor; and lawyer, lawyer. So it was with the brothers of Joseph.

What envy did to Joseph. Envy did not kill Joseph, but it did throw him into a pit. Reuben, as oldest brother, feeling responsibility for Joseph's safety, "delivered him out of their hands; and said, 'Let us not kill him . . . but cast him into this pit.'" Reuben evidently fully intended to rescue Joseph from the pit and return him to his father (vv. 21-22).

During dry seasons in the ancient Middle East, bottle-shaped wells with small openings at the top were ideal places of incarceration. Archeologists have found skeletons in such pits. The brothers stripped Joseph of his special coat, then tossed him into the well, perhaps intending to leave him there to starve.

Envy also sold Joseph into slavery. While Reuben was away temporarily, a company of Ishmaelites loomed in the east on their way to Egypt with balm and myrrh. Judah suggested selling Joseph instead of killing him. They lifted the lad from the pit and sold him for 20 pieces of silver. The merchants carried him to Egypt and sold him to Potiphar, an officer of Pharaoh and captain of the guard. Years later, when Stephen stood before the Sanhedrin, Stephen summed up the story, "And the patriarchs, moved with envy, sold Joseph into Egypt" (Acts 7:9).

T. DeWitt Talmadge suggested that envy kept an outstanding pastor out of his pulpit for a year. Dr. Albert Barnes, an outstanding leader of his day as well as author of a series of commentaries on the New Testament, known today as *Notes on the New Testament*, served as minister of the First Presbyterian Church in Philadelphia from 1830 to 1867. After a church trial, Barnes was decreed to sit silent for a year in the pew in his Philadelphia church while someone else preached. Talmadge commented that the pretended offense was that "Barnes did not believe in a limited atonement, but the real offense, the fact that all the men who tried him put together would not equal one Albert Barnes" (T. DeWitt Talmadge, *500 Sermons*, vol. 12, New York: Christian Herald Bible House, 1900, p. 188).

James wrote, "Where envying and strife is, there is confusion and every evil work" (3:16).

What envy did to Jacob. Envy broke Jacob's heart. When his sons brought back Joseph's special coat stained deliberately with goat's blood, Jacob recognized the garment immediately and concluded Joseph had been torn to pieces by a beast. Despite the attempts of his children to assuage his grief, "he refused to be comforted" (37:33-36).

Envy separated father and son for two decades. In his tear-stained memory Jacob could still see the ruddy-cheeked lad disappearing over the hill into the blue as he went off to seek his brothers. Little had he realized that that would be his last glimpse of his favorite son for 20 years.

Envy divided father and son. Envy has divided families, friends, churches, and even nations.

What envy did to the brothers. Envy hardened their hearts. After throwing Joseph into the pit, they sat down to eat bread, disregarding his pleas (v. 25). Around the table they plotted to sell him, probably thinking themselves righteous because they hadn't killed him.

Envy led them into duplicity. They had to pretend they didn't know how his special coat had become bloodied. They had to deceive their father into thinking an animal had devoured his favorite son, hypocritically weep and try to comfort him, and for over 20 years maintain the lie, and finally, confess it to Joseph before he revealed himself to them (44:28).

Envy gave them a disturbed conscience for over 20 years. Later, when Joseph accused them of being spies, "they said one to another, 'We are verily guilty concerning our brother, in that we saw the anguish of his soul, when he besought us, and we would not hear; therefore is this distress come upon us" (42:21).

A Greek story has it that when a statue was erected in honor of a famous athlete, a rival athlete was so envious that he vowed he would destroy that statue. So every night in the dark he chiseled at its base to weaken its foundation. He finally succeeded in making the statue fall, but it fell on him, crushing him. Joseph's brothers fell victim to their own envy.

How Envy Could Have Been Prevented

Noting how Jacob's family could have prevented envy will help us in overcoming envy in our own families and lives today.

By not playing favorites. Jacob should have known better than to have a favorite son. Favoritism had split his own family. He was the favorite of his mother, Rebekah, who urged him to steal the blessing which rightfully belonged to his brother, Esau, favorite of his father, Isaac. Forced to flee Esau's murderous wrath, Jacob had to suffer a 20-year separation from home, never to see his mother again, though he was later reunited with both brother and father.

When parents play favorites or make invidious comparisons between children, fertile soil exists for envy. They need to be careful to refrain from feeding natural sibling rivalry by displaying personal preference. A father, in response to the knocks of what he thought was his baby boy at his study door, called out, "Is that you, pet?" "No, it's only me," replied the older brother sorrowfully. That was the last time "pet" was used in that family.

In his book, *The Strong-Willed Child*, Dr. James Dobson says that where sibling rivalry exists, rules should be established and enforced fairly. For example, no sibling should ever be allowed to ridicule, tease, or harass another child. Each child should have some private space, either a separate room or part of a shared room. Children should not be required to play with each other when they prefer to play with others or be alone. Dr. Dobson also recommends mediating conflicts as soon as possible ("Some Tips That Might Help," *Leader Guidebook*, Summer 1978, p.13).

By not flaunting superiority. Joseph would have shown wisdom by not revealing his dreams in which his brothers bowed before him.

A person often unconsciously stirs up envy by flaunting his possessions or achievements. When a father spoke often of the accomplishments of his two sons—their degrees, careers, and honors—he galled several parents within earshot into envy. One lady aroused envy in others by frequent mention of her summer home, her furs, her round-the-world trip, her expensive jewelry. Those who wave their superiority say, in effect, "I'm the king of the castle" or, "I'm better than you." Some hearers will secretly wish to see them dislodged from their place or state of preeminence. They would do well to heed the words of the Apostle Paul. He advised, "Let us not be desirous of vain glory, provoking one another, envying one another" (Gal. 5:26).

By avoiding covetousness. The Latin word for envy is *invidia,* which paraphrased means "staring into." Joseph's brothers had probably spent a great deal of time "staring into" Joseph's status as a favorite son. Less curiosity over the fortunes, feats, fame, and fun of others plus more contentment with our own God-ordained niche will tone down envy. Victory over covetousness helps forestall any ill will against the possessor of the covetable item.

By accepting God's right to assign our place. Who makes people differ? If the brothers had recognized that Joseph's gifts proceeded from God who gives gifts to whomever He pleases, their acceptance of God's wise will in handing out privileges would have undercut their envy.

Too often our envy of another's superiority in some area is a subtle challenge to God's right to run His world and His work. Instead of resenting abilities of others, we need to be grateful for gifts conferred on fellow-believers. "How wonderful that my neighbor can sing so well!" "How fine that our friend's son gets such good grades!"

A classic example of willingness to take a secondary spot is John the Baptist. He realized that God had made him a voice, not the Word; a forerunner, not the Messiah; a herald, not the King. When he lost his crowds to Jesus, therefore, he humbly acknowledged Christ's divine appointment, "A man can receive nothing, except it be given him from heaven" (John 3:27).

If Joseph's brothers had understood that Joseph's leadership was God-ordained, they would have been willing to accept their inferior position, hard as that might have been. A couplet expresses it well:

It takes more grace than I can tell
To play the second fiddle well.

By love. Envy is first in the list of attitudes which are uncharacteristic of Spirit-produced love. "Love envieth not" (1 Cor. 13:4). Since ill will is an essential ingredient of envy, love, by annulling ill will, makes envy impossible. If the brothers had had love in their hearts for Joseph, they would have done no evil to the lad, for "love worketh no ill to his neighbor" (Rom. 13:10).

A sure way to love a person is to pray for him. On the 20th anniversary of his ordination, Andrew Boner wrote in his diary, "Envy is my hurt, and today I have been seeking grace to rejoice exceedingly over the usefulness of others, even where it casts me into the shade."

Later he wrote, "In my usual reading, in Genesis 37, I see how envy leads God to heap more blessing upon the envied one, and to withhold from the envier. Now this has been my fault in regard to brethren who have been blessed. I have sought to find reasons why they should not (be blessed). Lord, this day may I lay aside this forever. Give more and more to those brethren whom I have despised or thought unworthy of revival work."

When F.B. Meyer, the widely acclaimed British Bible teacher, first began visiting America to preach at Northfield summer conferences in New England at the invitation of D.L. Moody, he was greatly admired by the crowds. Then came the year his fellow countryman, Dr. G. Campbell Morgan, was also invited to Northfield. His excellent expositions attracted throngs away from Meyer. Not many knew it, but Meyer confessed there came the temptation to envy. But then he said, "The only way I can conquer my feeling is to pray for him daily, which I do." What chance has envy to remain in the heart of anyone who bears up before God the name of someone who seems more advantaged?

Later, when Meyer pastored in London, he heard that G. Campbell Morgan was coming to London to pastor a church. At first he strode the floor, greatly perturbed, convinced that Morgan would draw all his congregation from him. After much praying he won the victory, crying out, "Lord, fill Campbell Morgan's church so full it cannot hold any more, and then send the overflow to me!"

Prayer engenders interest and love; and love envies not. Perhaps we need to pray more often a litany found in the Book of Common Prayer: "From envy, good Lord, deliver us."

How to Face Adversity
Genesis 37:18-36; 39:1-6

With only two seconds left in a pro football game a few Novembers ago, the New Orleans Saints were losing to the Detroit Lions by two points. The Saints sent out placekicker Tom Dempsey to try a field goal which could win the game. But the ball had been spotted an almost impossible 55 yards from the goal post, plus 8 yards behind scrimmage, a total of 63 yards. Record for a field goal was 56 yards. Dempsey put his foot squarely into the ball with everything he had. When it cleared the crossbar by only inches, teammates, fans, and newsmen mobbed him.

The field goal was all the more remarkable because Dempsey was born with half a right foot. But as he grew up, he resolved to do everything other kids did, including 10-mile hikes with the Boy Scouts despite his handicap. In college he discovered he could kick a football farther than everyone he knew, but with just half a foot he seldom hit the ball dead center. But he kept practicing. One recent fall he was honored by the Professional Writers of America as the "most courageous player." Says Dempsey, a professing Christian, "Had I not been born with the handicap, I might never have become a field goal kicker and record breaker."

Joseph suffered adversity. He fell from favored son to slave. For the next 13 years, from the moment his 10 brothers pushed him into the pit until the day Pharaoh elevated him to second-in-command, he was a captive.

What tearing agony on learning his brothers were actually selling him to the Ishmaelites! Perhaps as the caravan moved toward Egypt, Joseph bargained with his owners, "My father is rich. Return me and he'll give you far more than the slave market." But they had no desire to get involved with a brokenhearted father who might turn revengeful. Besides, Hebron was too far out of the way. So Joseph looked back each day, hoping to catch a glimpse of his old father hurrying toward him. But Jacob didn't come. Joseph didn't know about the bloody coat.

In Egypt Joseph was exposed for sale in the open market. Placed on a platform, his foot chained to a block, naked except for loin cloth, Joseph stood there —a good-looking, healthy specimen. Prospective purchasers would pinch and poke, pushing down his chin to examine his teeth, as though he were an animal for sale.

Bought by an officer of Pharaoh, he trembled as he was led through the sphinx-guarded gate into the recesses of a strange but splendid palace. He was now the private property of Potiphar, who bore the title, "captain of the guard," equivalent of a "chief of the royal police." For the first few nights he would lie for a while in his cell, then rise and go as far as his chain would permit. He missed not only his father, but his five-year-old brother as well. In his loneliness he recalled the many times he had carried little Benjamin about, helping him walk and talk, and taking him to see any newborn puppies in the camp.

The record speaks of "the anguish of his soul" (42:21). Dying Jacob said of Joseph, "The archers have sorely grieved him, and shot at him, and hated him" (49:23). Amos spoke of "the affliction of Joseph" (Amos 6:6).

Like Joseph, we all have our captivities; we are trapped in one way or another. Some have been invalids for years, shut in by four walls. Others have been boxed in by accident, anxiety, disappointment, loneliness, illness, hardship, financial reverse, pain, misunderstanding, tragedy, or sorrow. With Joseph, all can say on occasion, "I never thought this would happen to me. I never expected to be captive in this situation."

Joseph was to suffer more adversity yet. False accusation by Potiphar's wife was to throw him into Pharaoh's prisonhouse, where he stayed for over two years with little prospect of ever getting out, much less of seeing his dreams come true. Leaving this episode for later treatment, let us note how Joseph faced the adversity of slavehood in Potiphar's household where, despite some degree of free movement, he was a virtual prisoner for about 10 years.

Sorrow

The brothers' consciences never let them forget the cries of Joseph. They later admitted to each other, "We are very guilty concerning our brother, in that we saw the anguish of his soul, when he besought us, and we would not hear" (42:21). Perhaps as these bearded brothers one by one looked into the pit into which they first threw Joseph, barely able to see the outline of his face and upraised hands, he appealed to them by name, "Judah! Asher! Simeon! Levi! Reuben!"

Or even as they sat down to eat, they heard his bitter cries to the invisible God of Abraham, who, he had been taught, would watch over him. But for Joseph no sound came, save the echo of his grief-stricken voice in that hollow well. Realizing he could not extricate himself without help, Joseph felt himself abandoned by both God and man. Perhaps he sobbed some more.

When Joseph was finally pulled out of the pit, he may have thought he was about to be released after some "brotherly" prank. But what anguish he must have felt when it dawned on him that he was being sold to merchants on their way to Egypt. The brothers never forgot Joseph's pleas for freedom.

Perhaps on his first nights in his cell in Potiphar's household he would vent his feelings, weeping and lamenting, "O God of Abraham, where are You? Send me back to my father. Can You hear me?"

It's not wrong to cry when adversity comes. A strange teaching suggests that even in bereavement no tears should be shed, citing the text, "that ye sorrow not, even as others which have no hope" (1 Thes.

4:13). If the comma is put in its proper place, however, there is no such restriction. The text should read, "that ye sorrow, not as those who have no hope."

Sorrow is natural. Jesus wept at the graveside of a loved one. Devout pallbearers made great lamentation while carrying Stephen to his burial (Acts 8:2). Widows cried aloud in their grief at Dorcas' death (Acts 9:39).

A young couple became the parents of a beautiful baby on whom they poured their love. But the baby took sick, and some time later, on a bleak wintry day, a little white casket was lowered into an open grave. The wind whistled across the cemetery during the brief committal service. Suddenly the mother shook her fist skyward, screaming, "God! Why did You take my baby? Why, oh why? God, I'll never serve You again." She collapsed in the back seat of the funeral car. A few days later she phoned her pastor, "I'm sorry for what I said at the cemetery. My world seemingly collapsed. For a moment I lost faith in God. But I've asked Him to forgive me. I'll be back teaching my Sunday School class before long."

Some tears, even momentary rebellion, often result from trouble's initial shock. But before long we must come to the place of acceptance, realizing that God is permitting it for a purpose.

Acceptance of God's Plan

After his first spasm of grief, Joseph turned to Him from whom his dreams had come, and who in some way would make them come true. He kept the promise of his ultimate elevation before him, trusting that somehow his incarceration was part of the divine plan. Even in his earliest weeks of adversity he must have reached the conclusion that what his brothers had meant for evil God would work for good.

Perhaps Joseph recalled the incident on Mount Moriah, as told to him by his grandfather Isaac. As little Joseph sat on Isaac's lap, the blind patriarch related how as a lad, tied to an altar by his father, God had stopped Abraham from plunging down the sacrificial knife, telling him to slay the ram just then caught by its horns in a nearby thicket. Perhaps Joseph reasoned, "If God was able to raise up Grandfather Isaac from what seemed an altar of death, then God can raise me up out of this captivity to that exalted position He showed me in my dreams."

When we find ourselves in Potiphar's house, beating our heads against a wall, it may well be God's place for us in His chain of events to lead us to His divinely chosen spot in the kingdom. Where we do not understand, we must submit, believing God has a purpose in it.

Rejection of Bitterness

Many react to adversity with resentment, then persist in unrelenting bitterness, blaming God and poisoning their soul. "If God were good, He wouldn't let this happen to me." They stop going to church and quit reading their Bibles.

A mother who lost her only child, a girl of six, shook her fist at God and declared war on heaven. Now and again she would go to the cabinet where her little girl had kept her toys. The mother would throw open the door, allow the toys to spill out on the floor, then, sobbing wildly, wave her hands over them. Her heart always bore an unhealed wound because she kept it festering.

How different from Job, who having lost wealth, children, and health, exclaimed, "Though He slay me, yet will I trust Him" (Job 13:15). Because of his submission to the divine will, Joseph would later take no revenge on his brothers.

Making the Best of the Situation

Picture Joseph in a strange country without friends, money, freedom, position, or knowledge of the language. He could have gone on for years, always saying, "No speak Egyptian." But, instead of moping around, he made the best of his situation, and set about to learn not only the language but the customs as well.

Though stripped of his coat, he had not lost his character. If he had to be a slave, he would be the best possible slave. He believed God had put him there and would some day make him a leader, so he determined to work hard to make his dreams come true. He performed the coarse, hard tasks assigned new slaves, jobs his father probably never gave him in his privileged capacity, such as cleaning stables or working in the field under the blazing sun.

Joseph was industrious, diligent, obedient, reliable, and conscientious. Just as he faithfully carried out his father's orders in tracking down his brothers, not content till he found them at Dothan, so he loyally executed Potiphar's assignments, busying himself, not loafing on the job. Sensing he was a slave of Jehovah as well as of Potiphar, whatsoever he did, he did it heartily as unto the Lord. No task was too menial. It was, as Leroy Phillips wrote, a matter of character.

It isn't the style nor the stuff in the coat.
Nor is it the length of the tailor's bill;
It's the stuff in the chap inside of the coat
That counts for good or ill.

As Joseph did the best he could in his captive condition, he discovered he had the favor of God. "The Lord was with Joseph . . . And his master saw that the Lord was with him, and that the Lord made all that he did to prosper in his hand . . . And he made him overseer over his house, and all that he had he put into his hand. And it came to pass . . . that the Lord blessed the Egyptian's house for Joseph's sake; . . . And he left all he had in Joseph's hand; and he knew not ought he had, save the bread which he did eat" (39:2-6).

Historians tell us the title *overseer* is a direct translation of an official position often found in the house of Egyptian nobility. Joseph had achieved the highest post possible as a slave. Realizing God was with him added to his confidence that some day God would fulfill his dreams.

If we find ourselves in a hard place, we need to make the most of our opportunities. Many handicapped persons have held positions of high responsibility. A fable tells of two grasshoppers who had been thrown into a pail of milk. One, sulking, "What's the use!" gave up and drowned. The other, kicking and working and making the best of it, churned the milk into butter, then walked off the top to freedom.

John Bunyan, jailed for preaching outside the established Church of England, made the best of his 12 years behind bars. Carving a flute out of the leg of the only stool he had, he made melody, and meditated on God's Word. He also wrote the unmatched allegory, *Pilgrim's Progress.*

Rough Edges

Somewhere along the line Joseph undoubtedly became aware of what has been termed his "bit of amiable self-conceit" which had exhibited itself in proudly wearing his special coat, and flaunting his dreams of self-exaltation. He saw that his flaw of pride needed to be checked by the rough treatment from his brothers.

Others with harsher judgment and less charitable language claim Joseph was a pampered child who without the adversity sent his way would have turned out a spoiled brat. In either case he realized that calamity had helped smooth the blemishes in his character.

In His providence the Lord may use affliction to correct us. Our love for Him may be cooling. He sees us trying to satisfy our souls with the comforts of life to which we are giving too much thought, energy, and time. So, He permits a jolt of pain to move us away from spiritual carelessness.

Stricken with polio, a man dictated the following from an iron lung, "If by means of sickness a man can learn his own weakness and dependence upon God, that sickness has been a blessing. If sickness can teach a man that life is more than physical, and character more important than the body, then sickness has been a blessing. If sickness can prepare a man to serve others better, then sickness has been a blessing."

Robert Browning Hamilton wrote:

I walked a mile with pleasure;
She chattered all the way
But left me none the wiser
For all she had to say.

I walked a mile with sorrow
And ne'er a word said she
But, oh, the things I learned from her
When sorrow walked with me!

The Apostle Peter suggested that just as fire refines gold, so trials test and purify our faith (1 Peter 1:7). A diamond has been described as a hunk of coal made good under pressure. Adversity may serve to make us more Christlike.

Making Much of God

Joseph knew it was God who caused him to prosper in Potiphar's household. He realized it was God who gave him favor in the eyes of his superiors. He was to reject Mrs. Potiphar's advances because he knew that to yield would be to sin against God. He later declared it was God who could interpret dreams. He knew in his heart that God would overrule the evil of his brothers to work out His purposes.

Though Joseph's body was imprisoned, his spirit was never shackled. His childlike, confident faith in God enabled him to face adversity successfully. He was conscious of the presence of God even though circumstances seemed to indicate His absence. God would triumph ultimately in his life. Joseph would wait patiently until the divine intervention.

In a dream a man saw himself walking along a beach with the Lord. Scenes from his life flashed across the sky. Each scene showed two sets of footprints in the sand. One was his, and the other belonged to the Lord. In the last scene he looked back at the footprints and noticed that many times along the path only one set of footprints registered in the sand, the other set suddenly disappearing for a while. He also noted that this occurred during times of adversity. So he asked the Lord, "You promised that You would walk with me all the way, but I notice that during the most difficult times of my life, only one set of footprints appear in the sand. When I needed You most, You deserted me."

The Lord replied, "Beloved child! I love you and would never leave you. During your times of trouble I carried you. That's when you see only one set of footprints."

Joseph Propositioned by Mrs. Potiphar
Genesis 39:7-20

The Bible speaks with utter frankness. It openly relates the story of how Joseph was propositioned by a woman of high rank and how he met the temptation.

Such openness has caused some critics to call the Bible an obscene book. But in no way does the Bible qualify for obscenity. Note the reserve, the reticence, the lack of details with which this story is told. What a contrast to the way sex is exploited in modern literature. Today's novelist is not content to handle sex subtlety, but rather depicts the whole gamut of immorality, dwelling in lengthy passages on its most vivid and detailed intimacies.

Whether or not a story is obscene depends on how and why it is told. If related to make a jest of sex, or excuse it, or to inflame the imagination, it is obscene. If told to show the wrongness of sin and its evil consequences, it is morally wholesome. The latter is the purpose of the Bible.

A doctor's medical book must deal with all types of disease. If the Bible, God's book on moral anatomy and spiritual disease, were to omit the so-called "impure stories," it would be defective. But a story like Joseph's temptation helps us cope with the moral plagues that beset us. All Scripture is profitable, not only for doctrine, but for instruction in righteousness (1 Tim. 3:16).

The Magnitude of the Temptation

Some Christians worry when tempted, "Am I weak? Do others get tempted too? And just as I am?" Paul wrote that every Christian is tempted, and in the same way as others. He also said that God would never let the temptation be too severe, but would always provide a way of escape (1 Cor. 10:13). Joseph was sorely tried, but came out victorious, and so may we if we understand what the temptation is.

This temptation appealed to a strong, natural drive. God, not *Playboy*, created sex. Along with everything else God made, He saw that it was good. Only its misuse—outside the marriage bond—is sin.

At 27, Joseph possessed a strong, normal sex urge. After suffering the life of a slave for 10 years, here was opportunity for sexual embrace. On top of this, he was a bachelor, often lonely, with little prospect of marriage.

This temptation came when Joseph was away from home. A good home acts as a restraining influence on the behavior of its children. But once they are away from home, emancipation may lead them to throw caution to the wind and succumb easily to the sinful charms of a wicked culture, especially if the person's piety is merely conventional. The veneer of civilization is so thin that voyagers just 10 miles out to sea often throw off moral restraint to indulge their immoral appetites.

Joseph, among a nation of idolaters, may have been tempted to think, "When in Egypt, do as the Egyptians do."

This temptation came from an important woman. Joseph was always someone's favorite. First his father's, then Potiphar's, now Potiphar's wife's. He was of beautiful form and handsome appearance (Gen. 39:6). The temptation was subtle, for it appealed not only to his natural appetite but to his ambition. Perhaps she might even plot to get rid of her husband, so that Joseph could take Potiphar's place, thus short-cutting his way to the fulfillment of his dream.

Should he not have been flattered by the attention of so important a woman? Refusal had its dangers. To deny her request could have gotten him into trouble with the boss.

This temptation came repeatedly. Not content with her lovely home, gardens, servants, husband, and position, Mrs. Potiphar coveted another man. She tempted Joseph, "Why work so hard? Take time off. Come rest awhile with me." When Joseph refused, she didn't give up. Painting her face with alluring cosmetics and donning lovely jewelry and pretty clothes, she persisted in her seductive invitation day after day. Though the Book of Proverbs had not yet been written, Mrs. Potiphar would certainly have fit the various descriptions of the strange woman whose flattering words lead to destruction (2:16-22; 5:3-11; 6:23-25; 7:5-27).

This temptation came with great opportunity. As chief steward, Joseph would have to pass through the inner apartments daily to inspect the store-rooms, usually located at the rear of the main house. One day when he was on necessary business, she grabbed him, and repeated the invitation. No servant was near, no one would see, and no one would ever need know. He could be home free. (Participants in sexual misconduct seem to forget the other party may gossip.)

This temptation came after elevation of position. After unusual blessing may come severe temptation. Following His baptism and His Father's voice of approval, Jesus was immediately led into the wilderness to be tempted by the devil. Here Joseph, after achieving a position of some honor, was faced with great solicitation to evil. A steady hand is needed to carry a full cup, and a firm balance to stand on lofty heights.

How Joseph Got Victory Over the Temptation

There's no sin in being tempted. Otherwise Jesus would have been guilty of sin, for He was sorely tempted. Temptation is not sin, but yielding is. Jesus never yielded; nor did Joseph in this temptation. Here are the ways Joseph secured victory.

He recognized that yielding would be sin. Joseph had a correct standard of right and wrong which much of our present generation does not possess. Books are filled with stories of wife-swapping, campus cohabitation, and various other forms of sexual immorality. Television and movies flagrantly show bedroom scenes of men and women unfaithful to their mates. A survey by *McCall's* magazine of 60,000 American women from all faiths and incomes indicated that 47% of them do not consider premarital sex sinful, nor do 27% deem extramarital sex wrong.

Joseph's view of yielding as nothing less than sin comes as a breath of refreshing air in the midst of modern moral pollution. He did not regard sensual indulgence as a necessity. Some counselors have been known to advocate sexual activity as a cure for emotional problems, but other counselors know only too well the damaging effects on the participants as they have tried to help pick up the pieces. The idea that immorality is the normal and expected thing is psychologically disastrous.

Joseph called this thing by its proper name," wickedness and sin" (Gen. 39:9). Not only would it hurt himself, but it would be a wrong against a fellow man, his master. In refusing his master's wife, Joseph pointed out how his master had committed everything he had into his hand. Gratitude to Potiphar for rescuing him from the slave market and for showing confidence in the ability of a stranger outweighed any sentiment his master's wife could stir in him (39:8-9).

The Decalogue's commandment against adultery (Ex. 20:14) protects a person's marriage. To be sexually involved with a neighbor's mate is to hurt that neighbor. Joseph knew that this woman belonged to Potiphar, and to yield to her temptation would be a blow against Potiphar.

Above all, Joseph saw it as a sin against God. His full description was "this great wickedness, and sin against God" (39:9). Mrs. Potiphar thought no one would see. But to Joseph the presence of God was more real than even that of his earthly master. To indulge would be iniquity in the sight of God to whom he would one day have to answer. Joseph's no to her was a yes to God.

He avoided temptation. Though Joseph had to enter the Potiphar house daily to perform his job, which subjected him to Mrs. Potiphar's repeated solicitations, he avoided her whenever possible.

If we pray, "Lead us not into temptation," common sense dictates that we should not court temptation but put as much distance between ourselves and temptation as we can. A man overcoming a gambling obsession found that he could not walk home by way of a certain street because he would have to pass a certain club where he had habitually gambled. A rehabilitated alcoholic admitted he couldn't have lunch in a certain cafe near his office because of his former practice of taking liquor with every meal he ate there. Because of the universal problem of evil-thinking, everyone needs to avoid pornographic novels, magazines, and movies. The computer formula, GIGO (Garbage In—Garbage Out) indicates a definite relationship between flirting with temptation and yielding to sin.

Staying busy. Joseph also avoided temptation by staying busy. Freudian psychology speaks of sublimation, the diversion of some instinctual impulse or desire from its primitive form to one more socially acceptable. We are told to take out our anger on a tennis ball or punching bag. One Christian leader said, "When an evil thought comes, I find that if I blink my eyes very rapidly, the thought is broken up. It is a voluntary act demanding voluntary attention; this draws the attention away from the thought. I thus catch my equilibrium and in that moment pray, 'Christ, save me.'"

Another man was troubled with an evil thought while walking through the forest. He deliberately picked up a heavy log and carried it back to the side of the path. This broke his pattern of thought.

Work can keep us from mischief. A seminary professor said that God calls some men to the ministry in order to keep them out of jail. A Turkish proverb points out, "Men are usually tempted by the devil, but the idle man positively tempts the devil." If the devil finds a man idle, he'll try to give him some work to do.

Joseph was about his business during the days of temptation, but Mrs. Potiphar was idle. Seven hundred years later, while lounging at home when duty dictated the battlefront, King David spotted beautiful Bathsheba and lusted after her.

He fled temptation. Though Joseph avoided Mrs. Potiphar as much as possible, one day, while on necessary business, he found himself alone in the house with her. When she confronted him directly, even grabbing his garment, he fled.

Victory in the Imagination

Joseph, anticipating this possibility, had planned in his mind that if ever she cornered him with her temptation, he would flee. A photographer, in Kenya to take pictures of elephants' habitats, had a close call with death when he suddenly realized an elephant was almost on top of him. Sensing a tusk right at his chest, he grabbed it with his left hand, the other tusk with his right hand, and swinging in between them, went to the ground on his back. The reaction was almost automatic, because time after time on the trails he had imagined himself trapped by an elephant's rush, and had planned what he would do. In this brush with death the elephant drove his tusks into the ground on either side of the photographer. With the elephant's curled-up trunk against his chest, he knew he could expect no mercy. The animal gave a wheezy grunt as he pushed down, rendering the photographer unconscious. Naturally he would have been crushed had not the tusks hit something in the ground that stopped them. The elephant, supposing his victim dead, went charging after the photographer's companions who had all scattered for cover. Commented the photographer, "I firmly believe that my imaginings saved my life."

Imagination is a powerful thing because it can lead to action. We dream about something, then do it. Pondering leads to performing. That is the idea behind advertising. A man pictures himself behind the wheel of a new car, then buys one. A lady imagines herself in a new dress, then shops for one. Inventions such as the electric light bulb, the airplane, and the ocean cruiser were once a blueprint in someone's mind. Likewise, crimes begin in the mind. The place to get victory over wrong is in the imagination.

A man who drank lake water was convinced he had swallowed a frog. When X rays revealed no frog, he still insisted there was a frog. His doctor consented to operate. Putting the patient into a mild sleep, the doctor made a superficial incision and placed a frog in a jar by the patient's bed. When the man awoke and saw the frog, he began to feel better immediately. Imagination had won the battle.

No one falls into sin suddenly. A mental landslide

precedes outer collapse. Someone said, "Sow a thought, reap an act; sow an act, reap a habit; sow a habit, reap a character; sow a character, reap a destiny." There's destiny in thought. Joseph's chaste thought life enabled him to resist Mrs. Potiphar.

Similarly, no one rises suddenly. When Joseph later stepped from prison into the chariot of second-in-command, the rise seemed sudden, but it was only the revelation of greatness he already possessed.

Early-stage Victory

Before the temptation could gather momentum, Joseph broke it up by fleeing. Though the New Testament was yet unwritten, he was putting into practice its command, "Flee also youthful lusts" (2 Tim. 2:22).

The best place to get victory is in the early stage. Three stages in a wrongdoing involve eye, foot, and hand. The first (eye) stage takes place when the imagination pictures some misdeed, as when a thief spots an elderly lady alone on a side street and pictures himself grabbing her purse. Second (foot) stage is his walk as he stealthily approaches the unsuspecting woman. Third (hand) stage is the actual grabbing of the purse.

Jesus warned that if our hand offends us, we should cut it off. If we've gone through the first two stages (imagination and approaching), and are about to perform some evil, we should immobilize our hand, and not do the misdeed. If we haven't advanced to the third (hand) stage, but are at the second (foot) stage, we should immobilize our foot to keep it from approaching any closer. "If thy foot offend thee, cut it off." But if we are in the first (eye) stage, just contemplating the wrong with our mind's eye, we should "pluck out our eye" by not thinking about it any more.

The best place to eliminate a rattlesnake is when it's still an egg, before it hatches. The easiest place to stop a snowball is before it rolls down a hill and gathers weight and momentum. Football players try to break up their opponents' plays behind the line of scrimmage, before the game gets going.

It is the same with temptation. Too many flirt with temptation, and fail to escape. A Chinese proverb puts it, "He who would not enter the room of sin must not sit at the door of temptation." Another saying puts it, "When you're looking at your neighbor's melon patch, you cannot keep your mouth from watering, but you can run."

A man used to go forward during every revival meeting to pray the same request, "O Lord, take the cobwebs out of my life." The preacher, tired of seeing him come forward repeatedly with the prayer, knelt beside him and prayed, "O Lord, kill the spider!"

The incidence of marital infidelity could be much reduced if married people would avoid slight, temporary intimacies with someone other than their mate. Indiscretion, if nipped in the bud, cannot grow into a serious situation. The wise and fore-armed will avoid taking the first step of carelessness.

One marriage counselor says that most infidelity begins in the mind, or if originally unplanned, wasn't checked in the mind stage. That's where our Lord placed the origin of immorality when He warned, "Whosoever looketh on a woman to lust after her hath committed adultery with her already in his heart" (Matt. 5:28).

In a candid article, *"The Traveling Man and His Wife,"* (*Bookstore Journal*, Sept., 1978, p. 22), well-known author Joe Bayly points out that wives must possess an attitude of trust towards their husbands absent on trips. And that husbands must merit that trust. Bayly, who spent years as a young Inter-Varsity staff member, visiting colleges and universities, counseling and spending time with young women as well as young men, did not find it hard to merit his wife's trust. Says Bayly, "I have never (except on one occasion years ago) been interested in another woman. She was a Christian student, the soul of honor, totally unaware of her attraction, and did nothing to encourage attention."

Bayly tells how he handled the situation. "When I realized that I was attracted to the young woman and was looking forward to seeing her, I stopped having any but the most necessary and perfunctory contact with her on campus or in meetings."

Even when a woman takes the initiative, Bayly believes "that a man can discourage attention and potential interest if he wants to."

The Christian is told to bring every thought into captivity to Christ, and to think on the pure, lovely, and virtuous (2 Cor. 10:5; Phil. 4:8). His mind can best be renewed by hiding God's Word therein (Ps. 119:11).

A medical doctor in London accepted Christ during the first Billy Graham Greater London Crusade. Before his conversion he was ruled by unchastity. His reading room was crammed full of filthy literature and pictures. But after his conversion he was repulsed by the thought of impure practices, so he promptly gathered up all his lewd literature, carried it to a London bridge, and tossed it into the Thames River.

When Joseph resisted Mrs. Potiphar's advances and fled, leaving his outer coat in her hand, she flew into a rage—"Hell hath no fury like a woman scorned." Imagine a Hebrew slave resisting Mrs. Potiphar. As Joseph hurried down the hall, the air was rent with mad shrieking. She yelled to the servants, "The Hebrew slave tried to assault me! When I screamed he ran away and left his robe!" When her husband returned she showed him Joseph's garment. Though he was angry at first (39:19), he may have realized Joseph was innocent, but to save face, tossed him into jail reserved for the king's prisoners.

Mrs. Potiphar seemed to get away with her immorality and slander. But she was in for a shock. The day would soon come when Joseph would be elevated to a position of second-in-command of all Egypt. She would then tremble at the possibility of his revenge. But regardless of Joseph, who likely never sought retaliation, she will still have to face a holy God at the day of judgment.

Could there be mercy for Mrs. Potiphar? Yes, if she asked God's forgiveness. And for all who have failed to resist temptation, we must never forget the words of Jesus to a repentant woman, who had been caught in the very act of adultery, "Neither do I condemn thee; go, and sin no more" (John 8:11).

5

More Trouble: Falsely Accused and in Prison
Genesis 39:20—40:23

When a pastor died, his widow commented, "Suddenly I lost my identity as a minister's wife. I lost my place in the community. I lost my home, a church-owned manse. Couples that had been close to Tom and me suddenly dropped me. All I had left was God."

Perhaps Joseph felt similar loss and loneliness when, stripped of his important position as overseer of Potiphar's household, he was bound and confined to the king's prison.

Joseph Suffered Severely

In his decade of captivity, Joseph had earned a fair degree of freedom, but now he was confined to a dismal prison. Two words are used to describe it. One literally means *round-house* (39:20-23). The other is the name Joseph gave it—dungeon (40:15). The prison was probably a windowless, stifling, smelly, and filthy, half-buried hall with a roof shaped like an inverted bowl. Through an opening at the top Joseph was lowered into the dank interior.

All day long the chains would clank monotonously as the prisoner dragged himself for a few steps of liberty. The Psalmist wrote, "Whose feet they hurt with fetters; he was laid in iron" (105:18, RSV).

He may have wondered temporarily, "Why be good? I resisted that evil woman, and see what I get!" Momentary disappointment enveloped him. "What about God's promise through my dreams of a place of leadership? Has God forsaken me? Must I spend the rest of my days in this hole?"

How did 27-year-old Joseph weather this situation when once again major adversity struck—false accusation resulting in incarceration?

Joseph Had a Positive Attitude

Though Joseph may have done a little questioning at first, almost immediately the lessons learned from previous adversity helped him again. Before long he bounced back to acceptance of this new trouble as somehow part of God's plan. There was no use nursing a grudge against Mrs. Potiphar. How silly to dissipate strength fretting because of evildoers. He agreed with the outlook of the psalmist who later wrote, ". . . evildoers shall be cut off; but those that wait upon the Lord, they shall inherit the earth" (Ps. 37:9).

No record exists of Joseph threatening any incrimination for the injustice done him. No cry of revenge escaped his lips, as far as we know, even though he was likely taunted by fellow prisoners over the charge of being involved with Potiphar's wife.

How prefigurative of Christ, who when "reviled, reviled not again; when He suffered, He threatened not; but committed Himself to Him that judgeth righteously" (1 Peter 2:21-23). To this same kind of nonvindictive behavior every Christian is called, when he finds himself the victim of false charges, unfair treatment, misunderstanding, or persecution.

As before, Joseph made the best of the situation. Again, he was industrious, faithful in whatever was asked of him. And again, the Lord was with him, giving him favor in the sight of the warden. Before long Joseph was given complete oversight over all the prisoners and their activities (39:21-23). Faithfulness in little items leads to larger responsibilities.

Joseph Helped Others in Their Predicament

Recently, bottles of poisoned wine were left on the doorsteps of three leaders of a major political party in Uruguay. None of the three men drank the wine, but one of their wives swallowed some and died minutes later.

Poisoning has been a popular mode of liquidation in all centuries. Two high officials of Pharaoh's court, chief butler and chief cook, were thrown into the dungeon, objects of Pharaoh's wrath as suspects in a plot against his life. Who would be in a better position to administer poison than the men who handled his wine cup and prepared his food?

One morning Joseph noticed their downcast faces. He could have shrugged the matter off, but instead he asked why they looked so sad. They told Joseph of their disturbing dreams which they couldn't interpret. (Each dream was rooted in the dreamer's occupation: the butler's with grapes, the baker's with cooked food.)

Joseph could have replied, "Oh, dreams. Don't pay any attention to them because they'll get you into trouble. Mine did!" But still with faith that God would fulfill his dreams, Joseph took the effort to interpret their dreams, giving credit to God. The butler would be restored; the baker would be hanged (40:6-22).

Adversity can be more creatively faced by extending assistance to others in their afflictions. By lending a helping hand to others even though suffering adversity himself, Joseph forged a link that led to later events.

A missionary couple in India sent their six little children to a school in the hill country. One terrible night the monsoon rains caused a river to sweep away the hillside cottage where the children lived, burying all six in its ruins. The parents were crushed by the seemingly purposeless tragedy. But when the first wave of grief subsided, they said, "Our six children are gone, so we must establish a greater family of neglected little ones." Gathering up abandoned children from the streets of Calcutta, they made a home for them. For more than 30 years they were parents to as many as 300 little ones a year.

The need for volunteer helpers in air-raid shelters and hospitals during World War II in England motivated many invalids to leave their wheelchairs and render valuable service to community and country. In helping others, they forgot their own aches and pains.

A seminary professor, the late Dr. William L. Stidger, at one time suffered a deep depression. During that period he didn't care about anything, for all seemed hopeless. A friend challenged him to think of all the people who had been a major help in his life, select one, then to write that person a note of gratitude.

Stidger thought hard. He recalled a school teacher who had given him a love of literature. So he penned her a letter, telling how she had inspired in him a love of great poetry and prose. Soon he received a reply in shaky handwriting. "Dear Willy, when I read your letter, I was blinded with tears, for I remember you as a little fellow in my class. You have warmed my old heart. I have taught school for 50 years. Yours is the first letter of thanks I ever received from a student, and I shall cherish it until I die."

A sliver of sunshine wedged into Stidger's mind, encouraging him to write another thank-you note, then another, and another, till he had written over 500. Thinking of others provided the therapy to heal his dejected spirit.

After the tragic flood at Toccoa Falls (GA) College in 1977 in which 39 people perished, a man who had lost his wife and two of his children was reflecting on why he hadn't done much weeping up to that time. "Every time I wanted to cry, someone needed attention and I was the first to offer. I was constantly looking out for the needs of the others and did not have time to think of myself."

When Paul was imprisoned in his own hired house at Rome for two years, he didn't sit back and mope about how badly God had treated him. Instead, he thought of others. He witnessed successfully to his guards who came from Caesar's imperial troops and won Onesimus to Christ and sent him back to his master. He also wrote Ephesians, Philippians, Colossians, and Philemon, and carried on a constant preaching and teaching ministry (Acts 28:30-31).

Joseph Tried to Help His Own Cause Along

When Joseph interpreted the butler's dream as a prediction of his restoration to his former position, he asked the butler to put in a good word to Pharaoh for him. "But think on me when it shall be well with thee and show kindness, I pray thee, unto me, and make mention of me unto Pharaoh, and bring me out of this house: for indeed I was stolen away out of the land of the Hebrews: and here also have I done nothing that they should put me into the dungeon" (40:14-15).

Did Joseph's request display lack of faith in God? Not at all. Trust in God does not rule out effort on our part. An old man who was raking leaves was asked if he didn't wish he could just utter a command which would make all the leaves suddenly assemble in a pile, ready to be burned. He surprised his questioner by saying he could do just that. Asked for a demonstration, the old man barked an order, "Leaves, jump into one pile." He then proceeded to rake the leaves into a big heap.

When Mordecai uncovered a plot on the life of King Ahasuerus, he was careful to have his name included in the record as responsible for saving the king's life. Mordecai's self-promotion later saved his life by bringing him to the king's attention at a moment when his own life was in danger (Esther 6).

When the decree to kill all Jews in the Persian Empire was proclaimed, Mordecai urged Queen Esther to plead with the king for the lives of her people.

Though he had faith that God would somehow save the Jews, Mordecai did not hesitate to exert every effort in that direction, even suggesting to Queen Esther that she had come to the kingdom for that purpose (Esther 4:1-4).

To try to change things that cannot be changed— our sex, abilities, and disabilities, for example—is futile. But the acceptance of the providential sovereignty of God in areas that can be changed does not mean passivity.

Paul did not take life lying down. When the Roman centurion was about to scourge Paul at Jerusalem, the apostle did not think it unspiritual to mention his Roman citizenship. Membership in this privileged group meant he could not be whipped. He did not miss the mind of God in helping his own cause (Acts 22:25-29).

A couple of days later Paul again used his energy to help God's will along. God's plan for him to testify at Rome had already been revealed to him in a night vision by an angel. When his nephew informed Paul of a plot on his life, Paul didn't answer, "Don't worry about the plot, young fellow, for the Lord has told me I'm going to reach Rome some day. We'll do nothing about it. Just fold your arms, relax, and God will work it out." Rather Paul called the centurion aside and asked him to bring his nephew to the chief captain, "for he hath a certain thing to tell him" (Acts 23:17).

After defenses before Felix, Festus, and Agrippa during his two-year imprisonment at Caesarea, Paul refused a trial back at Jerusalem. Because he knew he would be facing a "hanging jury" among his own people, he appealed to Caesar (Acts 25:9-11).

God's sovereign plan for us does not rule out our responsibility to help it along. He will not do for us what we can do for ourselves. When a youth group arrived at a camp to find it a shambles, the leaders said, "We'll trust the Lord. All will be fine." An associate objected, "We need to do more than trust the Lord. Things will not be fine unless we get busy." The campers got busy, and God honored their actions with a spiritually profitable camp.

Joseph Exercised Patience in Delay

When Joseph dreamed about the sheaves and stars bowing to him, little did he realize how many years would elapse before the fulfillment of those dreams. Here's an attempt to reconstruct the time sequence.

At 17 Joseph had his dreams and was sold into slavery.

At 27 he was falsely accused by Potiphar's wife.

At 28 he rose to prison-keeper.

At 28 he interpreted the butler's dream, asking him to put in a good word to Pharaoh. Then for two years he was forgotten.

At 30 he was suddenly remembered by the butler, setting in motion a chain of events that catapulted Joseph to second-in-command of all Egypt.

During the two disappointing years when he was forgotten, Joseph exercised patience. Since many prisoners held top positions in the royal household, he learned all he could about Pharaoh, the details of the government, the condition of the land, the location of granaries, the state of the crops. All this information, patiently acquired, would stand him in good stead in the immediate future.

The two-year delay caused by the butler's ingratitude was providential. Had the butler remembered earlier, Joseph might have been given his freedom, but not the rulership. He would have gone into obscurity, had events moved as quickly as he wished.

Abraham waited many years for the son of promise, Isaac. Moses waited 40 years on the backside of a desert after God's call to be the emancipator of His people. The night before wicked Haman was going to request the execution of Mordecai did the Lord awaken King Ahasuerus and cause him to reward Mordecai, thus saving his life. Jesus waited until His 30th year before entering His public ministry.

Lord Clive of England was a young man when he set out for India. A terrific storm swept his ship so far off course that it finally limped into a Brazilian port, where Clive had to wait months before getting passage to India. But during his long wait he learned the Portuguese language which qualified him on arrival in India for an important position with the East India Company. Ultimately the king appointed him Governor-General of India.

We need to remember that
God's help is always sure,
His methods seldom guessed;
Delay will make our pleasure pure,
Surprise will give it zest.
His wisdom is sublime,
His heart profoundly kind;
God is never before His time,
And never is behind.

—Anonymous

A patient spirit helps even in the small setbacks of life. A woman did a big wash, but when it was nearly dry, her line broke. All the wash tumbled to the ground. She did the wash all over again, afterward spreading it on the grass to dry. But a dog with muddy feet came along, frolicking on the clean white clothes. Instead of getting angry, the woman sweetly remarked, "Ain't it queer he didn't miss nothing?"

James said that we should count it all joy when we fall into adversity, for trials joyfully faced develop patience and maturity (1:2-4). Chastening produces righteousness; pruning yields fruit (Heb. 12:11; John 15:2). The two-year delay developed Joseph's patience, matured his spirit, steadied his character, and prepared him even more fully for the years ahead.

F.B. Meyer summed it up, "As a boy, Joseph's character tended to softness. He was a little spoilt by his father. He was too proud of his dreams and foreshadowed greatness. None of these were great faults; but he lacked strength, grip, power to rule. But what a difference his imprisonment made in him! From that moment he carries himself with wisdom, modesty, courage, and manly resolution, that never fail him. He acts as a born ruler of men. He carries an alien country through the stress of a great famine, without a symptom of revolt. He holds his own with the proudest aristocracy of the time. He promotes the most radical changes. He has learned to hold his peace and wait. Surely the iron has entered his soul!" (F. B. Meyer, *Joseph: Beloved–Hated–Exalted*, Old Tappan, New Jersey: Fleming H. Revell Co., n.d., p. 55).

6

Ruler over all Egypt
Genesis 41

There are some well-established facts about dreams. Everyone dreams several times each night, well over 1,000 times a year. The average dream lasts about 30 seconds. Though many seem much longer, most fade quickly, unremembered.

Some dreams stem from physical disorder, such as a cramped position of the body, too-heavy blankets, lack of fresh air, indigestion. A broken arm may lead to a dream in which a giant seems to be yanking on that arm.

Dreams are not voices from heaven, proclaiming truths about the universe or about the will of God. But they do tell us truth about our own inner feelings. A dream has been called a cartoon-like story of one's feelings or events, reflecting in some way things that have occupied our minds during the previous day or two. A tiger in a dream probably symbolizes someone or something we found frightening that day or the day before.

If you dream of a tidal wave about to destroy you, you should probably ask yourself what in your life seems overwhelming to you.

Or, one who dreams he is missing a train may be afraid he is not measuring up to something important. Dreaming of taking an exam may indicate fear of facing an ordeal unsuccessfully.

Many dreams are a message from us to ourselves. A man dreamed a close associate at work had died. On waking, and realizing it was only a dream, the man recalled he had never witnessed to his fellow business worker. Convicted, he made it his business to quietly share the Gospel with him. A dream should always be considered literally at first and examined for signs of objective truth such as warnings or reminders. If the dream makes no sense literally, then it should be seen as a possible metaphorical statement of the dreamer's feelings.

In contrast to visions which are supernatural, objective appearances that convey revelation, dreams are subjective commentary on our own feelings and attitudes.

Contrary to general notion, dreams are of little significance in the Bible, except in Genesis, Daniel, and Matthew. The only six specific dreams mentioned in the New Testament all occur in Matthew, and are confined entirely to warnings and announcements concerning the birth of Christ, except that of Pilate's wife, which concerned Jesus' trial.

Dreams played a significant part in the story of Joseph. They came in pairs. Joseph had two dreams about others bowing down to him. The butler and baker each had a dream. Pharaoh had two dreams, both with the same meaning. All six dreams could well have expressed the dreamer's feelings about current situations. For example, Joseph's dreams were related to his inner stirrings of incipient leadership, heightened by the favoritism of a doting father. Both butler and baker were thinking of their occupations and possible treatment by Pharaoh. Pharaoh's dreams could easily have stemmed from his fears of possible famine which Egypt suffered periodically. In any event, the Lord was involved in all these dreams.

Factors in Joseph's Rise to Power

Two years went by with innocent Joseph still in prison; two years of God's seeming forgetfulness as Joseph administered the affairs of the dungeon. Wouldn't the butler ever put in a good word to Pharaoh for him? The forgetfulness of man forced Joseph to rely on the memory of God. In due time the gears in God's plan began to mesh, so that the denizen of the dungeon became the premier on the throne. How did it happen?

Pharaoh's agitation. One night Pharaoh had two vivid dreams. In the first dream, seven fat cattle came out of the river, followed by seven skinny cattle, who then devoured the fat ones. In the second dream seven rich ears of corn grew on a stalk; then seven thin and blasted ears sprang up, consuming the fat ones.

The chief wealth of Egypt consisted of cattle and corn. The blasting east wind, dreaded by its inhabitants, would parch and shrivel corn, thus indicating a rainless season, which in turn resulted in a low Nile River, less food to eat, and loss of cattle.

Pharaoh's spirit was troubled (41:8). Was something serious about to happen? No wonder in the morning he sent for the so-called wise men and magicians to interpret his dreams.

The butler's intervention. Magicians played an important role in Egyptian life. These white-robed men, some old and bent, others young and vigorous, who moved soberly in twos and threes through the palace halls and gardens, were famous for their wisdom. But when Pharaoh told them his dreams, none could explain their significance.

As Pharaoh's anger began to rise, his voice rang through the hall. Wasn't there one among all the magicians who would interpret the dreams? Panic began to grip the wise men, for Pharaoh had been known to order the execution of incompetent magicians.

Suddenly, in the embarrassing silence, a court officer moved slowly forward, then meekly kissed the ground before the throne. All hushed to hear what the butler would say. Was this servant, who had been jailed just two years ago, going to risk his life by attempting to explain the king's dreams?

Signaled by Pharaoh to speak, the butler painfully recalled his falling-out of favor with the monarch, and perhaps just as regretfully his ingratitude to Joseph. "I do remember my faults this day; Pharaoh was wroth with his servants, and put me in ward in the captain of the guard's house, both me and the chief baker; and we dreamed a dream in one night, I and he; we dreamed each man according to the interpretation of his dream. And there was there with us a young man, an Hebrew, servant to the captain of the guard; and we told him, and he interpreted to us our dreams; to each according to his dream he did interpret. And it came to pass, as he interpreted to us, so it was; me he restored unto mine office, and him he hanged" (41:9-13).

When the butler finished his story, all eyes focused on the king. Pharaoh didn't hesitate. He ordered Joseph brought to him. Among the magicians could be heard the rustling of robes and the whispering of voices, "The dream to be interpreted by a Hebrew, a foreigner, a prisoner, a slave!" But Pharaoh was king and could do what he wished.

Joseph's interpretation. Though Joseph was brought hastily, he observed court etiquette by shaving and donning clean, white clothes. Amidst the thronged and breathless court, surrounded by the evil eyes of magicians who could little afford to surrender their prestige, Joseph heard Pharaoh say, "I have dreamed a dream, and there is none that can interpret it: and I have heard say of thee, that thou canst understand a dream to interpret it" (41:15).

Joseph humbly answered, "It is not in me; God shall give Pharaoh an answer of peace" (41:16). Joseph's confidence had been bolstered by God's previous help in correctly interpreting the dreams of both butler and baker. (And in a land that worshipped over 2,000 deities, Joseph would later doubtless seek opportunity to instruct Pharaoh about the one, true God.)

Joseph's answer pleased Pharaoh who proceeded to tell him his two dreams, ending again with the comment that he had told all this to the magicians but no one could explain.

More rustling and whispering among the magicians. "Will he reply? Will he dare speak when we kept silent?" They didn't have long to wait, for Joseph spoke immediately, as if guided by some higher power. "The dream of Pharaoh is one; God hath showed Pharaoh what He is about to do" (41:25).

Then Joseph explained that there would be seven years of plenty through all Egypt, followed by seven years of famine which would deplete the reserves. The doubling of the dream signified its certainty. But Joseph didn't stop with the interpretation. He added some urgent advice. "Now therefore let Pharaoh look out a man discreet and wise, and set him over the land of Egypt" (41:33). He included some directions for the storing of food in the plenteous years in preparation for the famine period.

The magicians looked at each other in amazement, not only because of Joseph's successful interpretation of the dream, but because of his boldness in making such specific recommendations to the great and terrible Pharaoh. But Pharaoh was pleased with the youth and his plan.

Sudden Elevation

Pharaoh asked his advisors, "Can we find such a one as this is, a man in whom the Spirit of God is?" (41:38) To execute such a plan would require a man of great wisdom. Even without his job resumé, which would have listed his several years of governing—as overseer over Potiphar's house, then over the king's prison—Pharaoh and his counselors agreed that no one was better fitted for the job than Joseph. So Pharaoh announced to Joseph, "Forasmuch as God hath showed thee all this, there is none so discreet and wise as thou art; thou shalt be over my house, and according unto thy word shall all my people be ruled; only in the throne will I be greater than thou" (41:39-40).

Then Pharaoh publicly invested Joseph with the premiership of Egypt. "Pharaoh took off his ring from his hand, and put it upon Joseph's hand, and arrayed him in vestures of fine linen, and put a gold chain about his neck. And he made him to ride in the second chariot which he had; and they cried before him, 'Bow the knee,' and he made him ruler over all the land of Egypt" (41:42-43).

Doubt has been cast on the historical accuracy regarding such a promotion. But Egyptian archeological discoveries tell of foreigners, including Canaanites, who achieved sudden elevation from slave to court official. (See Joseph Free, *Archeology and Bible History*, Wheaton, Illinois: Scripture Press Publications, 1950, pp. 76-77).

What a sudden transformation! From the depths of the dungeon to the steps of the throne. Hands no longer calloused by toil, but adorned by a ring. Neck no longer bowed beneath the disgrace of prison, but circled by a chain of gold.

Though his special coat had been ripped from his back years before, and though another garment had been snatched by Mrs. Potiphar, he was now enveloped in royal apparel. The investiture of a chief was a ceremony of considerable import, especially when the post conferred such high rank.

From rags to riches. From victim of envy to viceroy of Egypt. From the tomb to renewal of life. His story rivals the best plot of fiction.

Joseph was given a chariot in which to ride behind Pharaoh's. Others would have to walk in his presence. Runners would always warn others to get off the path for "Here comes Joseph!" Now the fulfillment of that boyhood dream of his brothers bowing to him seemed much more possible.

Joseph's rise illustrates the proverbs, "Seest thou a man diligent in his business? He shall stand before kings" (Prov. 22:29). And "Don't you know that this good man, though you trip him up seven times, will each time rise again? (24:16, LB).

The sign in a small business window read, "Boy Wanted." A lad was hired, given a few errands to run, then in midafternoon was sent up to the dingy attic, inhabited by mice and cobwebs. The owner said, "You'll find a long, deep box. I'd like you to put it in order. It's in the middle of the floor. You can't miss it."

The lad examined the box: old nails, screws, broken keys, and miscellaneous items. "Nothing worth keeping," he thought, "and besides it's cold and dark up here." The lad bounced down the stairs and was found an hour later loafing in front of the store when the owner returned. "Did you put the box in order?" "No, sir, it was dark up there, and I didn't see anything worth saving in the box." The lad was paid for his day's work and told his services were no longer needed.

The next day another lad by the name of Brown was hired. In late morning he was given the same assignment of putting the box in the attic in order. Just before closing he came down to the owner's office. He had gone without lunch. "I did my best, sir. At the very bottom I found this five-dollar gold piece."

As the owner said good night, he added, "I suppose you'll be back on the job tomorrow morning." After Brown left, the owner climbed the attic steps. What a thorough job Brown had done. He had made compartments out of pieces of shingles, labeling them, "Good screws," "Small keys somewhat bent," "Picture hooks," and so on. The owner chuckled to himself. "I've found the boy I want." Years later Brown became a partner. Then he inherited the business. The motto on his office wall read, "He that is faithful in that which is least is faithful also in much."

Jacob's dying blessing described Joseph as a fruitful tree by a well, "whose branches run over the wall" (Gen. 49:22). Joseph spent many years behind walls: in a pit, caravan, Potiphar's house, and prison, yet his blessings ran over the walls to save his family and an entire nation. All who drink deeply of the wells of God's grace will sooner or later overcome the barriers of life, to bring forth fruit that will bless others.

Joseph's Administration

Joseph had a job to do. To help him do it, he was given a new name, a bride, and limitless authority.

His name. Pharaoh called Joseph *Zaphnath-paaneah* (41:45) which meant, "the one who furnishes the nourishment of life." Historians tell us that in Egypt an office was titled, "Superintendent of the Granaries" (*Archeology and the Old Testament*, Merrill F. Unger, Grand Rapids: Zondervan Publishing House, 1954, p. 132). In view of the approaching famine, Joseph exercised this function in addition to his duties as ruler throughout all the land of Egypt.

His wife. Pharaoh gave Joseph a wife by the name

of "Asenath," daughter of Poti-pherah, priest of On (41:45).

His assignment. Pharaoh faded into the background. It became all Joseph who "went out from the presence of Pharaoh, and went throughout all the land of Egypt" (41:46) gathering and storing grain in the cities. When famine came, causing people to cry to Pharaoh for bread, Pharaoh sent them to Joseph to do his bidding. Joseph opened all the storehouses and sold to the Egyptians (41:53-56). He was an instrument to save countless people who otherwise would have had nothing to eat.

His kindness to other nations. The famine was widespread, affecting several nations neighboring Egypt. "And all countries came into Egypt to Joseph for to buy corn; because that the famine was so sore in all lands" (41:57). Joseph extended help to other peoples. And so it was a few years later that his own brothers came to Egypt for food and bowed before him.

Joseph as a Type of Christ

No student of Scripture can fail to see the many ways Joseph prefigured Christ. Both were falsely accused. Joseph was in prison with two others; Christ suffered on the cross between two thieves. Joseph announced that one of his fellow prisoners would go free, while the other perished; Christ proclaimed salvation to the repentant thief, while the other continued unrepentant.

Just as Joseph, after much injustice, was exalted to second ruler of Egypt, so Christ was brought from the grave after much insult and injury and placed at the

Father's right hand. Like Joseph, Christ has also been given a bride, the Church, composed mainly of Gentile believers. Just as Pharaoh placed the whole business of the grain in Joseph's hands, so the Father has committed all things into the care of the Son. As Joseph dispensed bread to save the lives of his own nation and of other countries as well, so Christ is the Bread of Life who dispenses spiritual nourishment to all nations.

Just as the Egyptians had to bow before Joseph, so we should bow before Christ now (41:43). Joseph's rise to power must have been hard on those who had been his enemies. How did Potiphar's wife feel when she heard of Joseph's elevation? When in court on important functions, seeing Joseph seated beside Pharaoh, how ashamed, speechless, even fearful, she must have been.

How did the butler feel? Perhaps badly at first on recalling his ingratitude and negligence. But he did remember Joseph and recommend him. So he could face the second-in-command happily.

How did the brothers feel when Joseph finally revealed himself to them, and his dreams came true? They had cast him into a pit to see what would become of his dreams. And now the dreamer was on the throne. Until things were made right, his presence would terrify.

If you had to face the risen, exalted Christ today, how would you fare? If, like Potiphar's wife you have slandered Him, or like the butler have neglected Him, or like Joseph's brothers have mistreated Him, get right with Him now.

During the coronation of the Queen in Westminster Abbey, just before the placing of the crown on her head, the Archbishop of Canterbury, as chief citizen in the country, called four times to each point of the compass. "I present unto you the undoubted queen of the realm. Are you willing to do her homage?" Four times a great affirmative shout thundered down the nave of the Abbey. Only then was the crown placed on her head. The hymnwriter reminds us that Christ is now presented to mankind as its undisputed King and Lord, and urges us to declare our allegiance,

> "All hail the power of Jesus' name;
> Let angels prostrate fall;
> Bring forth the royal diadem
> And crown Him Lord of all."

If we fail to acknowledge Him voluntarily in this life, we will be forced to do so in a future age. In that day every knee will bow and every tongue will "confess that Jesus is Lord to the glory of God the Father" (Phil. 2:11).

7

Preparing for the Years of Famine
Genesis 41:25-40, 46-49, 53-57; 47:13-26

The *National Geographic* carried an article, "Fearful Famines of the Past." In a severe famine in Italy in the fifth century, desperate people flung themselves into the Tiber River to escape the terrible pangs of hunger.

In an 11th century Near East famine, a single loaf of bread sold for the equivalent of $45; five bushels of grain sold for $250, and one woman gave a necklace worth $2,500 for a mere handful of flour. The caliph's stable, which had numbered 10,000 horses and mules, was reduced to three scrawny nags. Finally, in desperation, the people resorted to cannibalism.

Until the completion of the Aswan Dam in 1970, Egypt, whose area was 96 percent desert, had been particularly susceptible to famines. An old inscription contains the appeal of Pharaoh to one of his gods because of a terrible famine long before Joseph's time. "My heart is in great anxiety on account of misfortune, for in my time the Nile has not overflowed for a period of seven years. There is scarcely any produce of the field; herbage fails; stables are wanting. Every man robs his neighbor. The children cry, the young people creep along. The aged heart is bowed down; their limbs are crippled. The people of the court are at their wits' end. The storehouses were built, but all that was in them has been consumed" (George A. Barton, *Archeology and the Bible*, Philadelphia: American Sunday School Union, 1916, p. 305).

According to Joseph's interpretation of Pharaoh's dream, Egypt was in for a disastrous famine of seven years after a seven-year period of plenty.

The Principle of Plenty Followed by Famine

Feast is followed by famine. We see this in the economic world with its flow and ebb of prosperity and depression. Business volume is succeeded by recession. The market goes up, then down. We have the bulls and the bears. At the end of the booming post-World War I decade came the crash of 1929 and the years of hardship. Even though our government does its best to shield us from a similar disaster, the economy has its up-and-down cycles.

Feast follows famine in nature. Day is pursued by night. Light is succeeded by dark. Summer's long days are followed by the shorter days of winter when opportunity to labor is restricted. The fruitfulness of summer is gobbled up by the lean, barren winter.

The maxim of plenty followed by poverty holds true with regard to time. Youth looks forward to the many years yet ahead. Each day seems long, providing plenty of time to squander in play. But the psalmist, knowing that a famine would soon consume the years, advised, "Teach us to number our days, that we may apply our hearts unto wisdom" (Ps. 90:12). Suddenly, one day, at the end of high school we may discover that a quarter of our lives has sped by. By the time our children have grown up, it dawns on us that half of life has gone. For an older person the time between lunch and dinner seems like 15 minutes.

A man of mature years said, "I don't have much time left. I must gather up the loose ends. I must set my house in order. I must make my will." He had discovered that in relation to time, famine follows plenty.

The same holds true with regard to our strength. Children seem to have a boundless supply of energy. Some youth never seem to lose their pep. The Old Testament warns us to remember our Creator in youth before the evil days of decrepitude befall us, when knees shake, legs tremble, teeth fall out, eyes dim, and ears lose their hearing (Ecc. 12:1-4).

A man in a nursing home, leaning on a cane, bent in weakness, tells how he used to be a football full-back, blitzing through enemy lines for long yardage. Babe Ruth, sultan of the swat, spent his final years in a wheelchair.

Doesn't the feast and famine principle hold true for our intellect? In childhood, minds seem to learn so easily. Memory has its golden age in youth, absorbing with comparative speed. But as the years go by, a person discovers he cannot memorize as readily. Though mental powers do maintain their sharpness for many years, the time comes when they seem to diminish in power.

A young fellow says, "If I lose my job, I can get another." He's in those days of plenty with mentality keen, vigor full, and opportunities numerous. But after a certain age, if he loses his job, getting another won't be easy. The day of retirement will come to all, along with the discovery that the world is preparing to get along without us.

The years of surplus may be followed by years of scarcity in spiritual matters. Some reared in Christian homes and Bible-teaching churches with ample opportunity for Bible study, prayer groups, and Christian fellowship, suddenly find themselves in changed circumstances. Going to college, or changing jobs or residences, often removes these privileged folks from a Bible-teaching influence to a group that cares little or nothing for the things of God. They lose out spiritually. In every area of our country are people who would respond, "I know what you are talking about. I have tasted both environments, and the years of famine are upon me now."

The rule applies to money. A person who, saving up plenty for a rainy day, thought he had security, may discover that unemployment, major medical bills, and children's college tuition eat up his savings and leave him destitute. With no way to replenish his finances, and with worn out clothes making him look as if he had never known prosperity, the years of leanness have done their work.

Preparation for the Years of Famine

Surpluses are not meant to be wasted. "Waste not, want not." After the feeding of the 5,000 Jesus ordered the disciples to gather up the leftover fragments. A dozen basketfuls were gathered. After the feeding of the 4,000 they salvaged seven basketfuls. Industry has learned to utilize waste products. The blessings of health, intellect, strength, time, and money were never meant to be squandered, but to be conserved for confining experiences yet to come.

Joseph began to store up in the years of surplus so the nation wouldn't starve in the years of scarcity.

Before the famine. Joseph gathered up a fifth of the produce of the land during the productive years (41:34). One commentator suggests that since this was double the usual 10% tax, the fertility of the soil enabled them to give without complaint, or else adequate compensation was paid for the second tenth.

Joseph stored the grain in strategically located cities for easy access by every area. He toured the entire country, exercising his administrative ability. At first, he kept strict account. But when the grain piled up "as the sand of the sea, very much," he stopped counting, apparently making no more entries in the formal register (41:46-49). Incidentally, Joseph's storage of grain has been cited as among the earliest examples of banking (*Collier's Encyclopedia*, Vol. 3, p. 72, 1951).

Why didn't the people store up grain for themselves? Joseph's model should have prompted economy and foresight on their part. But despite warning of impending disaster, for seven years they apparently harvested bushels of golden grain, and used everything up, failing to store up reserves for future hunger. This human weakness of inability to deny present indulgence for future provision explains why one hard winter in the early years of the Pilgrims, Governor

William Bradford doled out daily a quarter-pound of bread to each person. Otherwise, he said, had it been in their own custody, they would have eaten it up all at once, and then starved.

During the famine. When the famine hit, Joseph opened up the storehouses not only to the Egyptians, but to the people of all countries in need (41:55-57).

At first he sold grain for money. When the people's money was used up, he exchanged grain for their cattle. When their cattle were gone, he sold them bread for their land and their own bodies (47:13-21).

After the famine. Allowing the people to work their former land, Joseph provided seed for sowing. In return, he exacted one-fifth of the harvest for Pharaoh.

Some consider Joseph's policy tyrannical. They accuse him of crushing his grovelling subjects to please Pharaoh and to aggrandize himself.

Others claim his actions were benevolent. In the first place, he gave full value of grain for whatever charge he made. His moving the people "to cities from one end of the borders of Egypt even to the other end" was not a policy to complete their subjugation, but to place them nearer the source of grain. When he took their cattle, he did them a favor, for now Joseph would be responsible for feeding the animals, quite a drain on any food supply. When the drought was over, he probably returned their cattle, and virtually farmed back the lands to the original occupants at the moderate rent of one-fifth of the harvest. Overall, the people did not deem Joseph oppressive, but rather applauded him, "Thou hast saved our lives" (47:25).

Using the Plenty of Today

In youth, prepare for the main years of life. A college student used to disappear after dinner each evening for uninterrupted, intensive study until he emerged at 10:00 P.M. for some relaxation and socializing. He earned high grades and later became a success in his field.

One leader testified that he owed much to a three-year period after graduation that he spent in obscurity in a minor position, for it afforded him ample time for additional study. These extra courses led later to increased responsibilities.

On the other hand, many students have shortcut their education, trying to slip by with two or three years of preparation when several more years are really required for that profession.

An English scholar who in his 70s, still received invitations from several American universities to give lectures, remembered the advice of his mother. When he was in his 20s, she said, "Son, you must not be content to prepare yourself for when you are 30, or even 40, but you must prepare yourself for when you are 60 or 70, should the Lord permit you to live." He made full use of his years of plenty to discipline his mind so that when the years of famine came, there was no lack.

The youth today need to develop good habits in the areas of eating, sleep, exercise, study, reading, time, and money. Most important, young people need time each day for meditating on God's Word, for prayer, and for memorizing Bible verses before it's so difficult to memorize, or even to read the Bible because of failing sight.

They need to establish the practice of regular church attendance, to develop and deploy their talents, and to cultivate a generous spirit. Mary, who took time to sit at Jesus' feet in the hours of plenty, was able to face the death of her brother, Lazarus, bravely and calmly in the day of famine.

Prepare for the late years. Parents who build good relationships with their children will reap rewarding friendships when they're older. Conversely, middle-life people should take time to enjoy their parents. For too soon their parents will be gone.

As a young, successful businessman, Herbert J. Taylor, originator of the famous Four-Way Test, was offered a position dealing with youth. Though his first love was youth work, an advisor urged Taylor to follow a business career. The advisor easoned that, as time went by, Taylor would be successful in business and able to give more and more time to youth activities. By the time he was 45, Taylor had gained control of a company and was able to devote increasing hours to youth projects. He had a share in the development of Young Life, Inter-Varsity Christian Fellowship, Christian Service Brigade, Pioneer Girls, and the National Child Evangelism Fellowship. These organizations all profited from Taylor's wise stewardship of ability and means in the day of plenty.

The need for setting aside a specific sum for retirement raises the whole question of how a Christian should spend his money. Admittedly, some people live too frugally, but most likely err on the side of overspending. We should begin by tithing—giving a tenth of our income to the Lord. One Christian couple, blessed by the husband's increasing salary, gave a second tenth, making their total contribution to the

Lord's work one-fifth of their income, the same proportion the Egyptians were required by Joseph to give.

Most, if not all, of our tithe should go to support our own Bible-believing church with its local program and missionary outreach. Extra monies could be given to one or more of the many Christian organizations doing a special worthy work for Christ.

Paul taught the principle of industry that we might have to give to the poor. "Let him that stole steal no more; but rather let him labor, working with his hands the thing which is good, that he may have to give to him that needeth" (Eph. 4:28). John Wesley's famous dictum was, "Earn all you can; save all you can; give all you can."

When we have given one tenth or two, we still haven't discharged our full responsibility. The remaining dollars belong to the Lord, and must be administered carefully as belonging to Him. We are required to support our family. Paul taught, "If any provide not for his own, and specially for those of his own house, he hath denied the faith, and is worse than an infidel" (1 Tim. 5:8). Family support includes, among other items, food, clothing, housing, medical and dental care, educational savings, recreation, cultural pursuits, insurance, and prudent foresight for a rainy day.

Futurists warn constantly that citizens of luxury countries are going to have to tighten their belts in the days ahead. As a result, a movement toward frugality and self-reliance, known as voluntary simplicity, has surfaced in the U.S. For example, the threat of a fuel shortage, plus increasing air pollution, has led many Christians to buy smaller cars.

In the final analysis, the spending of one's money is a personal decision, for which each will someday be accountable.

Prepare for eternity. Invited to a church service, a couple replied they were too busy preparing for retirement. Both husband and wife worked, saved all they could, never took a vacation, and spent weekends building a new, lovely house. One week before his 50th birthday, target date for retirement and move into their new home, the husband dropped dead of a heart attack.

Many claim, "I've prepared for the future. I carry hospitalization, even major medical. I have a substantial bank account in case of a rainy day. I'm insured heavily. Then when I'm 65, I'll get Social Security, and there'll be Medicare. So I'm all set." They have made excellent plans up to 65 and from 65 to death, but what about after death?

A grasshopper and an ant lived in the same field. All summer long the grasshopper jumped and made merry. But the wise little ant kept busy storing her food for the cold winter months ahead. The grasshopper laughed at the ant. "All you do all day long is work. Why don't you come and play with me?" As winter came on, the grasshopper grew cold and colder, and so hungry that one day he begged the ant, "Give me something to eat. I'm sorry I made fun of you." But the little ant replied, "Your chance is all gone, Mr. Grasshopper. The food I eat you wouldn't like. You should have been gathering your food in the summer, but you fooled away your life in the fields and now it is too late." The grasshopper went sadly away and soon died, for he hadn't used his day of plenty to prepare for the day of famine.

In Jesus' parable of the ten virgins, the five foolish ones squandered their chance to secure oil, so were left outside the wedding feast. But the five wise virgins took advantage of their opportunity to get a supply of oil, and were ready.

Now is the day of salvation when we can become followers of Jesus Christ and lay up treasures in heaven, before eternity is upon us.

Joseph's Wisdom Not His Own

Joseph acted with prudence only because his life was linked to God. Through God he learned of the coming famine, and from God he received wisdom that enabled him to save the nation.

For us to face the future, here and hereafter, we need superhuman knowledge and direction. How essential to turn our lives over to the Lord Jesus, the supreme Saviour, Master, Leader, Overseer, and Governor. This wisdom is illustrated by a truck driver who suddenly went blind as he drove his 40-ton car-transport rig along the Kansas Turnpike. As he hit his brakes, his truck, carrying eight new cars, began to weave from side to side. He called out a warning on his CB to traffic traveling behind him. The driver back of him came on the CB, "Take it easy. Get calm. Go to your right. You're on the shoulder. Back the other way." Then the comforting words, "You're okay now. Just shut it down." Said the truck driver, "I owe my life to that man."

People are hurtling down life's highway, blinded by sin, oblivious to the dangers ahead. They need direction from the Lord. They need to pray, "Jesus, Saviour, pilot me."

8

Joseph Reconciling His Brothers
Genesis 42:1—45:8

A police officer, directing traffic in a busy downtown, glared into the setting sun at oncoming traffic. A driver, thinking the officer was staring at him, pulled up and said, "Yes, I stole it," meaning the car, and submitted to arrest.

A father, hearing his son in the kitchen and wondering what time it was, called out, "Al, what is the big hand on?" After a pause Al replied guiltily, "A chocolate cookie."

Since 1811 Uncle Sam has been receiving anonymous sums of money as self-imposed fines for a variety of reasons, such as for taking Army blankets for souvenirs, or for deliberately failing to put enough postage on a letter. One widow, checking her late husband's books, discovered he had cheated the government, so she promptly mailed a check of $50 to the Treasury. All these monies have been placed in an account named the Federal Conscience Fund which now totals over three million dollars.

Conscience has been defined as God's watchdog and the court within man's innermost being. Someone wrote,

No ear can hear, no tongue can tell,
The tortures of that inward hell.

For a person to have peace, conscience must be reckoned with. Another put it,

There's a secret in his breast,
That will never let him rest.

Joseph's brothers may have thought that by selling him into Egypt, they were done with him. But they were so wrong. They had to confront him again, and deal with their dastardly deed. In the meantime they had no peace. For over 20 years their consciences bothered them.

When the famine became severe, Jacob, hearing corn was available in Egypt, sent his 10 sons down to buy grain. He kept Benjamin, his youngest son and Joseph's brother, who was now the apple of his eye.

As the brothers approached the borders of Egypt, things looked different. Instead of fields of waving grain, they saw ground baked and hard from the blazing sun.

Applicants for grain were screened by Joseph personally (42:6). One day Joseph's heart skipped a beat, for he saw his 10 brothers coming to buy. They bowed before him with their faces to the earth (42:6), a practice of homage and respect the Egyptians termed "the smelling of the earth." Joseph's dream of his brothers bowing before him was now fulfilled, though they didn't realize it at the moment.

They didn't recognize Joseph, for he had changed beyond recognition from a boyish teenager to a 39-year-old dignified ruler of Egypt. But Joseph knew the brothers, who were already men when they had sold him. They had changed little in 22 years.

Joseph had them at his mercy. How easily he could have punished them for what they had done to him. Should he torture them, then order their execution? Some suggest this was his supreme temptation—to get even by listening to their screams. But his princely character allowed none of that. Long since all desire for revenge had disappeared, indeed if he had ever harbored it.

What will he do, or say? How will the brothers find reconciliation?

Facing Their Wickedness

The first step to reconciliation with men (or God) is to honestly admit our wrongdoing. Joseph soon found out that his brothers had not genuinely acknowledged their gross misdeed.

Joseph began by calling them spies. They were reaping what they had sowed 20 years before, when they had doubtless considered Joseph's evil report to their father as an act of spying (37:2).

Their answer to Joseph's accusation indicated a failure to tell the whole truth. "Thy servants are 12 brethren, the sons of one man in the land of Canaan; and, behold, the youngest is this day with our father, and one is not" (42:13). True as far as it went, but how much was unsaid.

To prove they weren't spies, Joseph wanted one of them to go home and bring the youngest back, while the rest were detained in jail. Again the brothers were reaping what they had sowed, for they had been the cause of Joseph being detained in slavery.

But after three days Joseph changed his plans and

made it easier by releasing them, except for one, letting the nine return home with food. Over 20 years before the brothers had changed their plan to kill Joseph to the less severe fate of slavery. Joseph was now playing with them like a cat with a mouse. Only he had a good purpose in his wiles.

Joseph bound Simeon in the sight of the other brothers. Seeing their brother imprisoned, despite their pleas, reminded them of their mistreatment of Joseph many years before. For at this point they remarked to one another, "We are verily guilty concerning our brother, in that we saw the anquish of his soul, when he besought us, and we would not hear; therefore is this distress come upon us" (42:21). Then Reuben reminded them how he had urged them not to sin against the child, and how they would not hear (42:22).

Our sins, whether against our fellowmen or God, like chickens, come home to roost. A hit-and-run driver may escape the scene of an accident, but he will never escape the memory of the thud of the victim against his car.

A few months after beheading John the Baptist, Herod, on hearing of Jesus and His miracles, immediately reacted, "It is John the Baptist whom I beheaded." Joseph's brothers couldn't escape the phantom of wrong floating around them.

Maybe through the years the brothers hadn't talked much about their misdeed. When anyone broke their conspiracy of silence, the others would say, "Hush, don't talk about it. We showed father the bloody coat. He concluded he was dead, and wept. Let it remain buried." For 20 years they had been living a lie, trying to get away from their guilt, turning away from it, putting it out of their memories, being busy, but it always turned up to whisper in their ears at some most unwelcome time.

Genuine guilt cannot be disposed of that easily. It must be dealt with. The brothers had never honestly faced their cruelty, so Joseph determined to compel a full confession, far beyond the feeble, incidental reference to "one is not." They had never confessed to their father, to Joseph, or, really, to God.

Similarly, if we are estranged from someone, or from God, the first step is to face our transgression. God often has to put His finger on something deep in our life. God still convicts. Men still tremble. Ghosts still stalk. And they must be faced. What a pity if we were never confronted with the moral skeletons in our closets. Jesus made the Samaritan woman at the well admit to having five husbands plus her current cohabitation with a man not her husband.

A Genuine Change of Heart

The brothers, not realizing Joseph understood them, admitted some wrong, "We are verily guilty concerning our brother" (42:21). But Joseph wanted to test the depth of their anguish. True, their consciences had been awakened, but did they have a real change of heart, a different attitude, reflecting real repentance? Would they do the same thing over, or would they treat a younger brother kindly now? A poet expressed it:

> 'Tis not enough to say
> I'm sorry and repent

> And then go on from day to day
> Just living as we went.
> Repentance is to leave
> The sins we loved before
> And show that we did earnest grieve
> By doing them no more.

So Joseph set up a test to see if his brothers would forsake Benjamin, as they did him some 20 years before. Or, had they truly changed?

Back in Canaan the brothers explained to their father that Simeon was being held as a hostage till they brought back their youngest brother as evidence they were not spies. On emptying their sacks, each found his bundle of money hidden in the grain. In fear, old Jacob exclaimed, "Me have ye bereaved of my children: Joseph is not, and Simeon is not, and ye will take Benjamin away." But Reuben eloquently said to his father, "Slay my two sons, if I bring him not to thee: deliver him into my hand, and I will bring him to thee again" (42:36-37). Here was an advance hint of how this brother would meet Joseph's test.

When the corn ran out, Jacob told his sons to go again into Egypt for more. They reminded their father that they would get no more corn if they returned without their youngest brother. When Jacob lamented that they had ever mentioned their youngest brother, they replied that the ruler had directly asked about their family. Judah then volunteered to be surety for Benjamin. Since Judah was the one who had suggested selling Joseph into slavery, his vow of surety for Benjamin indicated a genuine change of heart (37:26-27; 43:8-9). Jacob, knowing it had to be, told them to take presents, plus double money in case the return of the first money was an oversight, and Benjamin.

Down in Egypt the brothers were ushered into Joseph's house. Afraid, the brothers offered to return the money found in their sacks, but the steward told them the money was from God. Then he brought Simeon out to them. A little later Joseph joined them, asking about their father, "Is he yet alive?" Gazing at Benjamin, his own flesh-and-blood brother, he had to hurry out to his private chamber, for he could not restrain his tears. Regaining his composure, he entertained them for dinner, seating them in order from firstborn down to Benjamin, who was given five times as much as any of his brothers. When Joseph had been the favorite with his special coat, the brothers were jealous. Now when Benjamin received special favor in the form of extra food, the brothers showed no envy whatever. They seemed to be passing the test.

When Joseph sent them home, he gave them all the food they could carry, plus their money, but he also hid his silver cup in Benjamin's sack. Before they had gone very far, his steward overtook them, asking why they had rewarded evil for good. Astounded, the brothers denied stealing the cup, offering to be slaves if the cup should be found in their possession, plus death to the culprit. The steward asserted that the guilty person would become his slave.

The steward proceeded to search from the oldest's sack to the youngest's, doubtless smiling to himself all the while, knowing where he would find it. When he found the cup in Benjamin's sack, that meant that Benjamin would have to return to Egypt as the steward's slave.

How would the brothers react to this test, contrived by Joseph, in which he constructed a scene similar to the episode of 20 years previous when the brothers had sold Joseph into slavery? Would they abandon their youngest brother Benjamin into slavery, as they had Joseph two decades before?

This time the brothers did not repeat the selfish betrayal. Two decades earlier they had turned a deaf ear to Joseph's pleas. Now they share in Benjamin's plight, and plead for his release. Judah, who two decades before had suggested selling Joseph to the Midianites, now makes a passionate appeal for Benjamin's release (44:18-34). His eloquent plea seemed to say, "Years ago we brought back a blood-stained coat to our father to let him think his son was dead, making our father mourn almost inconsolably. We have resolved never to repeat that deed. We will take this lad, Benjamin, back to his father, or we will not go at all."

The men who once sold Joseph into slavery would now choose slavery for themselves rather than return with news that would cause their father's death. Those who had thirsted for Joseph's blood now begged for Benjamin's favor.

Joseph had had enough. The brothers had passed the test with flying colors. Though they did forsake Joseph, they would not abandon Benjamin. Joseph was sure—his brothers were changed men, genuinely repentant.

To be reconciled to others whom we have injured, we need a change of attitude. Also, repentance toward a God we have offended is involved in divine pardon.

Acceptance of Forgiviness

Now it was safe for Joseph to grant his brothers forgiveness. He had seen their deepest feelings bared,
which indicated they were indeed sorry for what they
had done. Unable to control himself in the presence
of staff and servants, Joseph ordered them out. Then
he revealed himself to his brothers, "I am Joseph;
doth my father yet live?"

What a sudden blow! What a poignant scene as the
brothers shrank back in utter amazement and unbe-
lief! They stood, gazing like terrified animals. Who
was this that knew the name of their lost brother? And
yet it sounded like Joseph's voice! They were horror-
stricken. Their hearts pounded as their uneasy consciences piled a heavy burden on them.

They were speechless. The name *Joseph* struck terror in their inmost being! And ruler of Egypt! How
easily he could take revenge. How utterly cruel they
had been. They could expect no mercy. The record
says, "His brethren could not answer him; for they
were troubled at his presence" (45:3).

They did have an answer at their first audience with
Joseph when he accused them of being spies. "Nay,
my lord, . . . We are all one man's sons; we are true
men, thy servants are no spies" (42:10-11). But this
time, they had absolutely nothing to say. Their
mouths were closed. They were speechless.

Their terror must have been intensified when Joseph said, "Come near to me . . . I am Joseph your
brother, whom ye sold into Egypt" (45:4). Staring,
they seemed to see the face of the ruler change into
the face of their mistreated brother. No one but Joseph knew the secret. What will he do or say? Was

this the beginning of revenge?

Joseph answered their speechlessness. He allayed their fears immediately, for his next words were not of punishment, but of pardon and provision. He answered them in grace, telling them not to grieve nor be angry with themselves, for God had sent him before them into Egypt to sustain their lives, for five years of famine yet remained. He said, "God sent me before you to preserve you a posterity in the earth, and to save your lives by a great deliverance" (45:5-7). Continuing his forgiveness and looking at their misdeed through the eye of forgiveness, he said, "So now it was not you that sent me hither, but God" (45:8). What mercy!

Then he urged them to hurry home to tell their father the good news, and then to return with the whole family to dwell in Egypt, promising them protection and provision. In an act of deep reconciliation he embraced Benjamin, then weeping, kissed his 10 brothers.

Then "after that his brethren talked with him" (45:15). Their speechlessness disappeared, overcome by his answer. His words of grace took away the terror that had rendered them unable to talk. He doubtless told them of his two sons and the names he had given them. His elder, Manasseh, meant "forgetting," for God "said he, hath made me forget all my toil" and the loss of "all my father's house." The younger, Ephraim, meant "fruitful," for God "hath caused me to be fruitful in the land of my affliction" (41:51-52). Their conversation was animated and lengthy. Their tongues were now loosed in the atmosphere of pardoning love.

Joseph's forgiveness was full and free. That same spirit of willingness to forgive those, who have wronged us deeply, should be present in every believer. Newspapers around the country took note in January 1978, when Mr. and Mrs. Robert Bristol of Dearborn, Michigan, used part of their vacation to visit an inmate at the California Men's Penal Colony near San Luis Obispo. This prisoner had been found guilty of raping and murdering their 21-year-old daughter, Diane, in 1970 when she was selling encyclopedias door-to-door in San Diego. The Bristols felt the normal human reactions of anguish and grief, but they also knew that somebody had done something terribly wrong and needed the Lord. When the murderer was sentenced, they wanted him to know they had no hatred in their hearts for him, so arranged to meet him. The Bristols spent over three hours with him. At the end they embraced each other. The prisoner commented, "I'm not a born-again Christian, and I do not want to make that commitment until I can really mean it from the bottom of my heart—like you." To those who don't understand their actions, the Bristols reply, "If God can forgive acts like King David's sins of adultery and murder, I guess we can too. We don't condone the prisoner's actions, and realize he has a debt to pay to society, but we personally have forgiven him completely."

When we admit our wrongdoing to someone we have offended, he should grant immediate forgiveness. When we acknowledge our sinfulness to Christ, we have His promise of instant pardon.

But if we do not repent, some day we shall stand speechless before the Governor of the universe. But even now in this life a broken law should render every last member of the human race silent. Paul wrote that through the law "every mouth may be stopped, and all the world may become guilty before God" (Rom. 3:19). All stand without excuse before a holy God.

But Christ has an answer of grace. He came to answer the demands of a broken law by paying the penalty for our sins on the cross. When we receive Him as our Saviour and Pardoner, this grants us access into His presence. We can then, like Joseph's brothers, talk with Him in unhindered and uninhibited fellowship.

9

Joseph's Revelation to His Brothers

Genesis 45

During a war crimes trial in Germany, a former concentration camp guard was accused by the prosecutor of poisoning an inmate. The guard denied the charge, retorting, "It's my word against yours."

Then the prosecutor dropped a bombshell. "No, it's your word against the victim's. He recovered, and has been alive all these years, and is waiting in the side room to testify!"

When Joseph dropped his shocker on his unsuspecting brothers—"I am Joseph your brother, whom ye sold into Egypt" (45:4)—terror made them speechless. But Joseph dispelled their fright, as he told them about himself.

The Necessity of Joseph's Revelation

A man approached a preacher after a sermon. "I've a friend here who won't be satisfied till he hears something from your lips. He wants to know if I ever told you anything about him, or that I was bringing him to the service tonight." When the preacher answered no to both questions, the man continued, "I've tried for months to get him to church. Tonight he came for the first time. When the sermon was over, he was angry, accusing me of having told you all about him." The preacher turned to the stranger, "I do not know anything about you, sir, but there is Someone Else who does!"

The brothers did not recognize Joseph, but he knew all about the men bowed before him—their ages, characters, and record of misdeed against him. He amazed them by seating them around the dinner table according to age (43:33). Even though he hadn't seen Benjamin since he was about five, a little rosy-cheeked child running around Jacob's tent at Hebron, he could recognize his brother in this young man.

The brothers couldn't speak Egyptian, but Joseph understood their language. When they spoke among themselves about their mistreatment of Joseph many years before, and of their insensitivity to his cries of anguish, they didn't realize that Joseph comprehended their conversation (42:21-23).

Joseph had to at last reveal his identity to his brothers because they would not have otherwise recognized him. Similarly, if man is ever to know God, God must reveal Himself. The light of nature is insufficient. David Hume, the brilliant empiricist of the 18th century, once wrote an essay on the sufficiency of the light of nature for man's needs. F. W. Robertson, a noted minister, wrote an essay to establish the opposite conclusion, namely that the light of nature needed to be supplemented by the light of God. The two met to debate the point at the home of mutual friends. When Hume rose to leave at the end of the evening, Robertson took a light to show him the way. "Oh," said Hume, "I find the light of nature always sufficient. I can find my way alone." Upon opening the door, however, he stumbled over something and pitched down the steps to the street. Robertson, running after him, held his light over the prostrate philosopher and whispered softly, "You need a little light from above."

In reality, man does not seek after the light of God (Rom. 3:11). God does the seeking. When Adam sinned, the Lord went hunting him, calling, "Where art thou?" (Gen. 3:9) Self-righteous Saul got the surprise of his life on the Damascus Road when in answer to his question, "Who art thou?" he received the reply, "I am Jesus whom thou persecutest" (Acts 9:5). After the conversion of Zacchaeus, who on the surface seemed to be seeking Jesus, Jesus' comment was, "For the Son of Man is come to seek and to save that which was lost" (Luke 19:10). Any seeking we do is really the result of His seeking us. "We love Him, because He first loved us" (1 John 4:19).

We didn't knock on heaven's door, asking Christ to come down to earth to be our Saviour. He took the initiative. Unless God had revealed Himself, humanity, like the superstitious Athenians, would have forever worshipped at the altar of the unknown God.

Joseph yearned to reveal his true identity because he knew how much his brothers needed him: first, to clear their consciences, and second, to provide food for the five remaining years of famine. The situation would be so severe that people wouldn't bother to put the plow in the ground (45:6). Even before revealing his identity, he ordered their sacks filled with abundant food, and their money returned.

Similarly, Christ longs to make Himself known to people whose consciences are stained with sin's guilt. Even before sinners repent, Jesus treats them in kindness, in common grace making sun and rain to fall on the evil as well as on the good.

The Content of Joseph's Revelation

What message did Joseph carry? Simply that for many years he had suffered on their behalf. He had been sold into slavery, worked in Potiphar's household, then endured shame and humiliation. Though innocent, he had been numbered with the transgressors and cast into prison. Though his brothers, then before him, were responsible for starting him on the road to suffering, great good had resulted. Joseph, utterly magnanimous in forgiveness, reconciled his brothers back into happy relationship with himself.

How like Christ who suffered untold agony on our behalf. Our sin brought Him to the cross, wrapped Him in shame, and caused His suffering and death. Now risen and ascended, He offers reconciliation. Perhaps in no other quality does Joseph more fully typify Christ than in the mercy extended to those who wronged him.

Further, Joseph's message was one of full storehouses for those who lived in the land of famine. Likewise, the Gospel of Christ speaks of spiritual plenty, abounding grace and glory, and an inheritance incorruptible, undefiled, and unfading for those made heirs of God and joint-heirs with Jesus Christ.

Also, Joseph's message spoke of a home for the brothers and their families. "And thou shalt dwell in the land of Goshen, . . . and all that thou hast: . . . and ye shall . . . bring down my father hither" (45:10, 13). Christ's Gospel brings with it the promise of a heavenly home: "In My Father's house are many mansions" (John 14:2).

Hunger drove these brothers down to Egypt. The storehouses of God's grace and glory are only for those who hunger after forgiveness and thirst after righteousness.

The Obligation of the Brothers

To carry Joseph's message with haste. The word "posthaste" dates back to the days of Henry VIII, when some messengers with mail irresponsibly stopped on the road to play games or dilly-dally in some other way. Therefore, a law was passed decreeing death by hanging for any dispatch-carrier who delayed the mail. Thus letters of the 16th century were often ornamented with a drawing of a messenger suspended from the gallows with this admonition printed beneath, "Haste, post, haste! Haste for thy life!"

Joseph gave this order, "Haste ye, and go up to my father, and say unto him, 'Thus said thy son Joseph, God hath made me lord of all Egypt. Come down unto me; tarry not.'" Joseph repeated the command to haste (45:9, 13).

Commenting on Dr. Martin Luther King's assassination in 1968, a Californian said, "Before he was buried, a postman delivered to my home a copy of Life Magazine with a cover picture plus nine pages about his life and death." Then he added, "Two thousand years ago the Lord Jesus died. After His resurrection He commanded His disciples to tell the whole world of His love, suffering, death, and untold treasures of spiritual wealth. Yet nearly 2,000 years later, a third of the world's population has not been effectively confronted with the Gospel."

To carry Joseph's message with authority. Their message was, to begin with, "Thus saith thy son Joseph" (45:9). Their communication bore the authority of the lord of all Eygpt.

Hundreds of times the Bible contains the expression, "Thus saith the Lord." Neither theories, homespun philosophies of men, nor opinions of leaders, but the authoritative, infallible Word of God is the message needed today.

A short man, wishing to drive a nail into a wall to hold a large picture, stood atop a wobbly box he had placed on a chair. Balancing himself precariously, the man gave the nail a few hesitating taps with the hammer. "Why don't you give a brave blow or two, and settle it?" his wife asked. His answer, "How can a man give a strong blow when he's standing on a shaky foundation like this?"

Anything less than a sure "Thus saith the Lord" will not provide a firm enough foundation for declaring the divine good news.

To reinforce the message with their personal experience. The brothers were to back up the message with personal testimony. "And ye shall tell my father . . . of all that ye have seen" (45:13). They had visited a palace where there was no want of food, had sat in person at the governor's banquet table, and had tasted Egyptian dainties "enough and to spare." From personal experience they could confidently declare the truthfulness of their words.

Effective communication of the Gospel requires firsthand tasting of the Bread of Life. We must have sat at the Governor's table in order to tell of all the spiritual bounties available. Those who carry the Governor's message must first be genuinely nourished in His presence.

To use the provision provided for the task. To bring back all the members of the family from Canaan to Egypt "Joseph gave them wagons, according to the commandment of Pharaoh" (45:21). Several would have been required to transport the 70 people in the family. Joseph also gave the brothers provision for the trip back to Canaan, changes of clothing (five changes to Benjamin plus 300 pieces of silver). To his father he sent 10 donkeys laden with the good things of Egypt, and 10 female donkeys laden with corn and bread and meat for his father on the return trip (45:21-23).

These provisions helped motivate Jacob to undertake the trip to Egypt, for " . . . when he saw the wagons which Joseph had sent to carry him, the spirit of Jacob their father revived: and Israel said, 'It is enough: Joseph my son is yet alive: I will go and see him before I die'" (45:27-28).

To carry out His commission to be witnesses to the ends of the earth Christ has provided the promise of His presence, and the power of the Spirit (Matt. 28:18-20; Acts 1:8).

To carry it without quarreling by the way. Joseph gave this parting advice, "See that ye fall not out by the way" (45:24). Did he know his brothers too well?

Were they not the same men who had fallen suddenly on the Shechemites to kill them? Though they had undoubtedly undergone a change for the good, the old, unpredictable, ferocious natures still lurked not far below the surface, giving Joseph some concern lest something happen along the way.

Joseph realized that his brothers would now have to confess to their father both the cruel deed they had perpetrated against himself, and the deception they practiced on Jacob for over 20 years. Dreading the ordeal could have easily led to bickering and recrimination along the way. Reuben might have asserted his innocence, "I tried to save Joseph. Judah, it was your idea to sell him." Judah might have retorted, "But everybody else agreed. And Reuben, you went along with the plan of spilling goat blood on Joseph's coat." Joseph wanted to forestall arguement on the trip.

How sad that people engaged in the all-important task of proclaiming Christ's revelation should have fallouts along the way, splitting into splinter groups over trivial, inconsequential points. How tragic to see believers with great promise, having served well for part of the distance, slip by the wayside and end up on the shelf, like Demas whose love of this world led to his departure from Paul (Col. 4:14), and probably from the Lord. Paul said he kept his body under control lest he should become a castaway (1 Cor. 9:27).

Are you becoming more enamored with this world system? Do you have some little resentment against a sister? Some litle chip on your shoulder? Have you been hurt by a brother? Are you out of sorts with someone in the church? Go seek forgiveness. Get right with each other. As ambassadors of the Governor, we are in too notable a business to get sidetracked.

The Need for Personal Dealings

The brothers could not have taken advantage of Egypt's abundance without personal contact with the governor. No one else was permitted to dispense the bounties. Says the record, "Joseph was the governor over all the land, and he it was that sold to all the people of the land" (42:6). Pharaoh had issued the decree, "Go unto Joseph; what he saith to you, do" (41:55).

The brothers had headed for Egypt without any interest in the governor, intending to merely buy corn, fill their sacks, then return without personal dealing with any ruler. They went as if going to a store, carrying money to make a purchase, not to meet the owner. But they discovered the necessity of dealing with the governor personally.

Too often people try to get spiritual "goodies" apart from a personal relationship with Christ. They attend church, go through liturgy, sing hymns, submit to ordinances as mere ritual, and make the motions of prayer and worship without having any direct dealing with the Lord Himself. They deem Christianity a set of rules, a collection of ideals, a round of ceremonies.

But a personal relationship with Christ is part and parcel of genuine Christianity. The benefits of His grace cannot be secured by any indirect means whatever, not through any church or its ministers, but through Christ, the only Mediator between God and man (1 Tim. 2:5). The doctrine of the priesthood of believers teaches that any individual can come to Christ directly, apart from any intermediary.

Joseph's brothers could have learned all about the storehouses in Egypt, their number, dimensions, capacity, the quality of the corn, and the description of the men in charge of each granary. But all such knowledge would have availed nothing if the brothers hadn't made a direct appeal to the governor himself.

How easy to glory in Bible knowledge, quote verses from memory, discuss great doctrines, talk about the size of our sanctuaries and denominational differences, and not know Christ personally.

A minister, calling on a newcomer to the community, was greeted by a mother, "My daughter here has been a great church worker; she gave all her time to her former church, and now has moved here." Then the daughter told the minister what a great church she came from, their form of service, type of organization, and all about their wonderful preacher. When she finished her recital on the glories of her church, the minister ventured to turn the conversation in a personal direction, asking, "Tell me something of your personal experience with Christ."

She replied, "I—I don't know quite what you mean."

He asked what she knew of the person of Christ. Again came her reply, "I don't understand."

Then the minister asked, "Have you ever really met Christ? Do you know Him as your Saviour?"

She stammered, "Well, I—I hope so. I'm a member of the church, you know."

The minister replied, "That's not the question. I'm

asking whether you have personally, as an individual, had direct dealing with the Lord Jesus Christ. Have you received His word of forgiveness? Do you know anything of the joy of walking with Him?"

Her only reply was, "I belong to another denomination. I guess we see things differently."

She talked all about the storehouses of her religious Egypt, but she did not know the Governor.

To be forgiven of their nasty deed against Joseph, his brothers had to have a personal confrontation with him. Without this personal reconciliation none of the bounties of Egypt would have been given the brothers, nor would their guilty consciences have been cleansed. All benefits centered in the governor.

The blessings of salvation come through personal dealings with Jesus Christ. We may be terrified and speechless at what He knows about us, but personal repentance and faith in Christ will bring His words of reconciliation. Also, our spiritual provisions are wrapped up "in Christ" with whom God also freely gives us all things (Rom. 8:32).

When we get to know Christ in this personal way, the Stranger of Galilee becomes our Elder Brother.

Joseph and His Father
Genesis 45:25—49:33

During World War II a father in the U.S. received a telegram that his son with the Allied forces in Europe was missing in action. Some items, supposedly his son's belongings, were sent home. When the war ended and a decade went by, the father had long since assumed that his son was dead. Then suddenly one day came word that his son was alive. He had been the victim of amnesia and of a mix-up in identification. What a joy to learn he would soon see his son.

Such was the case of Jacob who for 22 years had deeply mourned for his favorite son, whom he thought had been mauled to death by a wild beast. Suddenly he learned that Joseph was alive and, unbelievably, a ruler in Egypt.

Why didn't Joseph contact his father immediately upon his elevation? Some think Joseph's failure in this respect was a definite blot on his character, for how could a devoted son let his father go on in sorrow, thinking his boy dead. Whatever Joseph's fault, it was but a fraction of the crime of the 10 brothers who caused their father's grief and let him wallow in it all those years.

But how did Joseph know his father thought him dead? He had no idea of the story his brothers had concocted to explain his absence. Joseph may have wondered why his father hadn't come looking for him.

Very likely Joseph had little opportunity to contact his father. His was a mammoth, time-consuming job—collecting, storing, and dispensing grain to keep a nation from starving. He simply could not spare weeks away from his work.

Some argue that Joseph could have dispatched a messenger to tell Jacob that he was alive, but such news might have incited revenge by the father on the brothers. Also, didn't Joseph's dreams indicate his family would some day bow down to him? Joseph suspected that sooner or later the famine would drive the brothers down to Egypt to come knocking at his door for grain. Then he could seek reunion with his father.

Joseph's love for his father comes through strongly in his contacts with his brothers. On their first trip to Egypt, how eagerly he listened to their mention of the youngest brother and their father (42:13). On their second journey his first question was, "Is your father well, the old man of whom ye spake? Is he yet alive?" How glad he was to hear that not only was he alive but in good health (43:27-28).

Whatever Joseph's reasons for not communicating with his father, his repeated inquiry about his father's welfare displays filial affection undimmed by nearly a quarter of a century of separation. Because he yearned to see his father, he pressed the brothers to bring Jacob and all the family back to Egypt to live.

Let's look at the story from Jacob's viewpoint.

A Leaden Sky

Jacob summarized his earthly sojourn, "Few and evil have the days of the years of my life been" (Gen. 47:9). Repeated trials crossed his path. After stealing Esau's blessing he had to flee for his life, never to see his mother again. For 20 years he was cheated by his employer—Uncle Laban, who palmed the wrong wife off on him, then made him work seven more years for the right one, and who decreased his wages 10 times. Calling this period "affliction," he said, "In the day the drought consumed me, and the frost by night; and my sleep departed from mine eyes" (31:40).

With great difficulty he escaped from Laban, then risked reconciliation with a potentially revengeful Esau. He suffered a thigh injury in a wrestling match with an angel. He was in danger of a reprisal attack by the Canaanites after his sons tricked and slew the Shechemites. He suffered the staggering blow of the loss of his favorite wife, Rachel. Then came the climactic tragedy when his sons brought back Joseph's bloodstained coat, sending him into inconsolable sorrow.

Incidentally, some of his troubles Jacob brought on himself. Years before, he had deceived his father; now his sons deceived him. He had deceived his father about his favorite son, Esau; now he is deceived about his favorite son, Joseph. To deceive his father, Jacob had used goatskin to pretend he was hairy; now his sons used the blood of a goat to pretend Joseph had been killed. What Jacob had sown he was certainly now reaping.

Even though over 20 years had gone by, Jacob's sky was covered with clouds. Every time he recalled kissing Joseph good-bye and watching him disappear over the hills, a knife cut through his heart. How often he took out the special coat, "I made him this special robe. He was my favorite boy. It's been torn and soaked with blood. Some beast has devoured him. He's gone, gone forever. I shall go down to my grave mourning."

The sun had disappeared from his sky. The years passed with little relief. Shadows deepened into despondency over his missing Joseph. When his sons returned from their first visit to Egypt, the darkness intensified, for they came back without Simeon who was being held hostage till they brought down Benjamin. Jacob, bent under the unrelenting ache of many years, lamented, "Joseph is not, and Simeon is not, and ye will take Benjamin away. All these things are against me" (42:36). Yes, few and evil were his days.

Our world contains thousands of Jacobs, whose skies, for one reason or another, are overcast. Family situations, marital problems, loss of job, accident, financial reverse, loss of child, or wayward children, have coated the heavens. That bloodstained coat of some bitter, perhaps bereaving trial, throws a mantle of gloom over the late evening hours of life.

A Rift in the Clouds

Suddenly a ray of light glimmered through a rift in the sky. The brothers bombshelled Jacob with the news that Joseph was alive and governor over all Egypt. Jacob couldn't believe it.

"But we've seen him," the brothers insisted. "We've talked with him. He had a banquet for us. We sat at a table with him. He placed us in order of our age. Remember how we brought our money back after the first trip? That was Joseph's doing!" So eager to tell the good news, the brothers almost interrupted each other.

Jacob searched their faces, trying to catch every syllable, thinking it all a dream. His voice and hands trembled, "Joseph's been dead these many years. The dead don't come back!"

Almost in chorus the brothers responded, "But he's very much alive. He's become a great man. He's governor over all Egypt. He lives in Pharaoh's palace!"

Trying to believe, Jacob exclaimed, "If he were alive, he'd come to see me!"

"But he's a busy man," the brothers replied. "He's in charge of all food in Egypt. The famine's too great for him to leave."

Then the brothers added, "Joseph has sent some gifts. Come outside the tent and see." Jacob looked. The rift in the clouds grew a little bigger. Jacob saw 20 donkeys loaded with the good things of Egypt. "Father, this food Joseph sent for you to eat along the way as we all go back to Egypt. And see these wagons. These are to carry all our family down there. You know, father, we don't have wagons like these in Canaan. See the large, heavy wheels that look like wooden discs."

"And look at the clothes he gave us. And Benjamin's. He gave him five changes of raiment and 300

pieces of silver. Remember how he used to play with
Benjamin!"

Jacob's spirit revived. "It is enough. Joseph my son
is yet alive. I will go and see him before I die." The
rift in Jacob's sky grew large. The sun began to shine
through.

About this time the brothers had to swallow their
pride and confess their cruelty that had landed Joseph
in Egypt. But they were quick to add, "Joseph told us
not to grieve, nor be angry with ourselves, for God
sent him into Egypt to save our lives and preserve our
posterity. Father, we did terrible wrong, but Joseph
has forgiven us. God overruled our evil for good."

Though this was another awful blow to Jacob, the
rift in his clouds grew bigger. More sunshine splashed
through.

The Brilliant Sun

Jacob met Joseph. As the group of 70 neared the border of Egypt, Jacob's pulse beat faster. For Joseph
also the intervening weeks of anticipation were full of
feverish anxiety. When he heard that the patriarch
had reached the frontier of Egypt, he readied his
chariot to meet his father. Then from Jacob's caravan
the cry went up, "Joseph is coming!" Weary Jacob
strained his eyes at the approaching train of travelers
to get a glimpse of his long-lost son. Then from the
midst emerged a bejewelled ruler in a long robe who
fell on Jacob's neck and wept for a long time (46:28-
30).

The intense delight of reunion compensated for
much of the heartache of two decades of separation.
Proudly looking his governor-son over from head to

foot, Jacob cried, "Let me die, since I have seen thy face." But the Lord had more sunshine in store for Jacob.

Jacob was introduced to Pharaoh. A great social gulf separated the sovereign of Egypt and the shepherd of Canaan. Joseph could have refrained from bringing Pharaoh and Jacob together. But the reunion seemed to make Joseph once more a lad, basking in his father's affection. So Joseph, still unashamedly a son to Jacob, delightedly presented him to Pharaoh.

Sad to say, some children do not so honor their parents. One high school girl, embarrassed by her mother's scarred cheek, deliberately looked the other way when her mother passed near a group of her high school friends, hurting her mother deeply.

On the other hand, a young man whose shabbily dressed mother had put him through college by taking in washing, and was at his graduation ceremonies, walked down to her, placed the diploma on her lap and a kiss on her furrowed cheek, exclaiming, "Mother, you really earned it."

Jacob blessed Pharaoh. Twice Jacob blessed Pharaoh (47:7, 10). Pharaoh showed his high regard for Joseph by granting his family territory in the land of Goshen, located in the eastern part of the Nile Delta, one of the richest sections of Egypt. An Egyptian inscription indicates that frontier officials often permitted Canaanites to enter this part of Egypt in periods of famine (Merrill Unger, *Archeology and the Old Testament*, Grand Rapids: Zondervan Publishing House, 1954, p. 134).

The choice of Goshen was providential for many reasons. The isolation provided opportunity for the handful of 70 to develop into a large nation. In Canaan, tribes would have exterminated them had they begun to grow big.

This new environment enabled them to escape the contamination of the Canaanites whose gross immorality was a major reason the Lord later told the Israelites to obliterate them completely.

The seclusion of Goshen permitted them to carry on their occupation of shepherding.

Their separation also protected them from the idolatry of Egypt, which boasted over 2,000 gods.

Their location on the border nearest Canaan would make for an easier exodus four centuries later.

With the capital of Egypt in Joseph's era situated in this area, Jacob would be close by for both protection and visiting (International Standard Bible Encyclopedia, p. 3153).

A Continuing Sun

Jacob lived in Egypt for 17 prosperous years. His family gained possessions and "multiplied exceedingly" (47:27-28). Doubtless Jacob and Joseph had frequent times together, but two visits before Jacob's patriarchal blessing (chap. 49) are specifically mentioned.

Near the end of his life, Jacob requested Joseph to vow he would be buried, not in Egypt, but in Canaan with his forefathers (47:29-31).

Then when Joseph heard Jacob was sick, he came to see him. Jacob strengthened himself and sat up in bed. Finding that Joseph had brought along his two sons, Jacob proceeded to bless them, placing his right hand on younger Ephraim, who would be greater than older Manasseh (48:8-20).

At this point Jacob gave a significant thanksgiving,

as he addressed Joseph. "I had not thought to see thy face; and lo, God hath showed me also thy seed" (v. 11). How like God to do exceedingly abundantly above what we ask or think.

Moses' mother, fearing for the life of her new baby, hid him in an ark of bulrushes. Not only was his life spared, but he was adopted by Pharaoh's daughter into the royal family. Moreover, Moses' mother was paid wages to move into the palace and rear her own son (Ex. 2:1-10).

Hannah wanted a son so badly. For a while it seemed her prayer would never be answered, but God gave her not only one son, but four sons and two daughters (1 Sam. 1:1-23; 2:21).

Naomi lost her husband and sons. With bitterness she returned to Bethlehem, thinking she would never have any descendents. But through a loyal daughter-in-law, Ruth, who married her relative, Boaz, Naomi found herself in the lineage of the Messiah (Book of Ruth; spec. 4:17-22).

The dying thief asked merely to be remembered by Jesus at some future time when He came into His kingdom. But Jesus replied that the thief would, that very day, be with Him in paradise (Luke 23:39-43).

The prodigal son intended to ask to be only a hired servant. But his rejoicing father freely forgave all, put on him the best robe, a ring, shoes, killed the fatted calf, and made merry (Luke 15:20-32).

In salvation, our Father doesn't just forgive us our sins, leaving us pardoned criminals, but declares us justified. He not only gives us the status of never-having-sinned, but adopts us into His divine family. Where sin abounds, grace does much more abound.

Jacob, who despaired of ever seeing Joseph alive, deeming him dead for over 20 years, now saw not only Joseph, but Joseph's sons as well.

In the liturgy for the presentation of his tithes and firstfruits a Jew was supposed to say, "A Syrian ready to perish was my father, and he went down into Egypt, and sojourned there with a few, and became there a nation, great, mighty, and populous" (Deut. 26:5).

The Jacobs who live under leaden skies need to remind themselves that the game is not yet up. Joseph may yet be found. Judah may yet straighten up. The problem that caused the mourning may yet be resolved. The sun still may shine.

One New Year's Eve several men gathered in a bar where liquor flowed freely. Samuel, the local minister's son, was mildly intoxicated. The town skeptic entered. "They're having a watchnight service over in the church. Let's have one here." Taking a drink, he turned to one of the group, "Brother Jones, will you please lead in prayer." It was a perfect imitation of a preacher's tone. Jones caught up the joke, dropped to his knees to give a mock prayer.

"Now let's sing a hymn," the skeptic continued. The others joined in noisily. When the boys were finished, he turned to Sam, "Brother Sam, your father is the town preacher. Why don't you preach us a sermon for our spiritual good?" Again he imitated a preacher's tone.

The idea was disagreeable to young Sam. He tried to run out, but the men stopped him. They threatened, "Preach a sermon, or you must treat every man here." Sam, broke, agreed to say a few words.

"Try the text, 'The spirit is willing but the flesh is weak,'" shouted the skeptic. So Sam started out in a mumbling manner, saying that in spite of their good intentions they would find out that the flesh was indeed weak. And that unless they made a break with their old sinful past as the New Year was about to begin, they would all end in destruction. It came out so strongly that the town skeptic sneered, "Why, I think the fool's in earnest."

Something in the skeptics's words grabbed hold of Sam. He began to say things which had been in his heart for months but were stifled by his wicked life: parts of his father's sermons, fragments of prayers uttered by his long-dead mother, verses he had learned in Sunday School. As he began to speak with force and sincerity, his audience looked surprised, resentful, then quite interested. Seeming to sober up, they listened in silence.

Sam's words began to affect himself. He thought, "If these things are true, then why don't I get down on my knees and pray to God for mercy?" Finally, he did just that, right in the middle of the bar floor.

Two others became Christians that night. Though the town skeptic never made any profession of faith, he was never again heard to mock Christianity. Sam related later, "As I turned the corner on my way home, I overtook my aged father, feebly making his way home from the watchnight service. What happiness when I took his arm and told him that his prayers had been answered. He spent the rest of the night on his knees, thanking God."

The doctrine of the resurrection was fore-shadowed in Jacob's reunion with Joseph whom he thought dead for over 20 years. Though Jacob's years up to then were full of trouble, the best was yet to be after the reunion with Governor Joseph, not only for the next 17 years but for all the world to come. Because of the resurrection of our glorious Governor Jesus Christ, we shall discover that "the sufferings of this present time are not worthy to be compared with the glory which shall be revealed in us" (Rom. 8:18).

11

Dispelling Doubts about Forgiveness
Genesis 50:1-21

A letter to a religious question-and-answer column asked, "I made a decision to trust Christ for forgiveness over 30 years ago, but it doesn't seem real to me. I have prayed so often. Will you please tell me how I can be perfectly sure that I am saved?"

Campus Crusade questionnaires filled out at the first session of its many training institutes through the years indicted that 10 to 25 percent of their enrollees were not sure, at the start of the course, that they then possessed eternal life.

Doubting one's forgiveness is a spiritual problem with a long and widespread history.

Joseph's Brothers Doubted
The Bible says, "When Joseph's brethren saw that their father was dead, they said, "Joseph will peradventure hate us, and will certainly requite us all the evil which we did unto him" (50:15).

About 17 years before their father died, Joseph had thrown his arms around the 10 brothers who had cruelly sold him into slavery, kissing them with tears of joy, and telling them not to grieve because God had overruled their evil deed to save their family from starvation.

Perhaps their fears were dulled during the weeks of the funeral proceedings. After 70 days of mourning, including the 40 days for embalming, came the long trek with the coffin back to Canaan. The procession, large and unusual, included officers of the court, Egyptian elders, and all the adult members of Jacob's family, accompanied by chariots and horsemen. The proud aristocracy of Egypt willingly followed the corpse of a shepherd Jew to his final resting place out of honor to his son. At the burial site Joseph "made a mourning for his father seven days" (50:10).

Hardly had the retinue returned to Egypt than the brothers feared the possibility of Joseph wreaking vengeance on them. Perhaps they viewed him in awesome light, dressed in the dazzling white robe of Egyptian officialdom, with fingers bejewelled and carrying his ivory walking stick.

They may have reasoned, "Joseph didn't punish us when he revealed himself to us because he wanted to get Father down to Egypt. And he wouldn't hurt us as long as Father was alive. But now, with Father gone, he'll probably take some horrible retaliation which he has been dreaming up for years."

They felt this way despite the years of Joseph's protection and provision in the land of Goshen. Were not these day-by-day reminders convincing proof of his kindness? Perhaps the brothers recalled how Uncle

Esau, cheated out of his blessing just before his father Isaac died, made the threat, "The days of mourning for my father are at hand; then will I slay my brother Jacob" (27:41). Expecting a repeat, they muttered among themselves, "Soon as the days of mourning are over, Joseph will get even with us."

Not daring to approach him themselves, the brothers sent a messenger to Joseph to plead their cause. Some think the messenger was Benjamin, who had done nothing needing forgiveness, and who as Joseph's only full flesh-and-blood brother would have ready audience with the governor. The messenger bore this petition, "Thy father did command before he died, saying, 'So shall ye say unto Joseph, Forgive, I pray thee now, the trespass of thy brethren, and their sin; for they did unto thee evil; and now, we pray thee, forgive the trespass of the servants of the God of thy father'" (vv. 16-17).

Did Jacob give such a command? Though the brothers could have made up the story to buttress their petition, it's entirely possible that before Jacob died, they told him their fears and received this advice.

Then the brothers came in person, falling down before Joseph's face (again fulfilling his boyhood dreams of their prostrations before him). Begging for mercy, they offered to be his slaves.

Many Christians at some time or other doubt their forgiveness. Even young men studying for the ministry at evangelical schools have been known to question their salvation. Though they had the promise of forgiveness years before, as well as enjoying the Lord's fellowship in the meantime, they begin to wonder if they are really forgiven.

Some doubt is normal, even healthy, for resolved doubt strengthens faith. But to continue in a state of uncertainty, wondering, "If I were to die, or if Christ were to return, would I be saved?" makes a person feel wretched. Lack of assurance also paralyzes Christian service. Many reason, "If I'm not sure I'm going to heaven, why bother to tell others how to get there?"

When the world famous San Francisco Golden Gate Bridge was under construction some decades ago, several workmen lost their lives by falling from precariously high positions. Consequently, the work was proceeding much too slowly till someone hit upon the idea of building a net under the construction area. Then, any workman who fell would not tumble to his death, but be caught by the net.

So a giant safety net of stout cord was made and swung under the construction work, (the first time in the history of major construction that such a net was used). The cost was reportedly about $100,000. The work then proceeded at a much faster rate because the workmen knew that if they did slip, their lives would be spared. They could work without the dread of uncertainty.

Joseph's brothers had become uncertain of their forgiveness, making them fearful and miserable.

Reasons for Doubt

Why, after nearly two decades of Joseph's kind treatment, did the brothers feel they had to beg Joseph not to repay their evil?

Insufficient knowledge. When the brothers sold Joseph at age 17, they never saw him for about 22 years, till he was around 39. Then after their reunion they may not have seen much of him, for between them was a great gulf. Their lives had little in common. They were rough-and-ready Syrian peasants concerned with cattle and pasture in Goshen. He was involved in high affairs of state at Pharaoh's luxurious court.

Though the brothers had learned much about Egypt's customs and climate, and much about Joseph's authority and administrative ability, they hadn't discerned his gracious character. They didn't perceive that he was forgiving, kind, compassionate, and unrevengeful. They imagined Joseph's goodness stemmed from his respect for his father, but hadn't grasped that his love was unconditional and came straight from his heart.

One reason some Christians doubt their forgiveness is a deficiency in their knowledge of Christ. Though they can recite many of His sayings and speak of His miracles, they are hazy on His character. Knowledge of the person and redemptive work of Christ helps us trust Him more. He was the preexistent member of the Trinity, who voluntarily came down to earth to die for us on the cross. His resurrection evidenced the Father's acceptance of His sacrifice at Calvary. He now lives to intercede for His own, therefore able to save everyone who comes to God through Him.

Joseph's brothers hadn't learned that nothing could separate them from Joseph's love. Believers' doubts can be overcome through the realization that "neither death, nor life, nor angels, nor principalities, nor powers, nor things present, nor things to come, nor height, nor depth, nor any other creature, shall be able to separate us from the love of God, which is in Christ Jesus our Lord" (Rom. 8:38-39).

Believers, forever gathering information from the news media, friends, and books, need to turn more to their Bibles to learn of the Saviour who is full of grace for sinners, and who loves us to the very end.

Circumstances and feelings. The brothers thought Joseph's conduct was governed by the circumstances of their father's presence. Their father's absence was Joseph's opportunity for revenge.

People too often look to circumstances for assurance of forgiveness. If things go badly, they doubt God's goodness. But peace never comes through analysis of our experiences or in a long list of divine providences. These may well provide stimuli to faith, but not its basis.

Nor should we go by feelings. If we do, faith will fluctuate as feelings fluctuate. One day we'll feel forgiven; another day, we'll feel unforgiven. When a person says, "I don't feel forgiven," he should remember that spiritual justification is a divinely legal, forensic act, a pronouncement of God that declares us forgiven and in God's family, regardless of our feelings.

When bride and groom say, "I do" to each other, the preacher's pronouncement of marriage still holds true day after day, even if the bride wakes up one morning and feels unmarried. It's a matter of record, not feeling. Similarly, when a person says yes to Christ, then the Father pronounces that person forgiven, a declaration that holds true regardless of the person's fluctuating feelings. Martin Luther wrote,

> For feelings come and feelings go,
> And feelings are deceiving;
> My warrant is the word of God,
> Naught else is worth believing.

> Though all my heart should feel condemned
> For want of some sweet token,
> There is One greater than my heart
> Whose word cannot be broken.

The enormity of the crime. When Joseph's brothers threw him into a pit, then sold him to the Midianites, they might not have thought they were doing anything terrible. Was not the dreamer getting his just desert for his delusions of grandeur?

But as their father's grief didn't lessen with the passing of time, they began to realize the extent of their cruelty. Though treated kindly by Joseph, an increasing sense of the awfulness of their crime made them wonder how Joseph could possibly have forgiven them.

Though some sorrow for sin is present at conversion (else we wouldn't have sought pardon), the passing of years often makes us see the magnitude of our earlier sins in deeper hue. New discoveries of our past, or even present depravity, may disturb us. How could a holy God forgive such sins which now loom in darker shadow? People have been known to leave Christian service because they could not dislodge from their memory bygone iniquities.

When the brothers, sensing the enormity of their ruthlessness and doubting Joseph's forgiveness, asked pardon a second time, they dishonored his earlier, gracious act. Similarly, we dishonor Christ by coming back to ask forgiveness over and over.

A little boy conducted a burial service for his favorite cat. Tenderly placing the corpse in a shoe box, he cut a hole in the lid so the tail could protrude up, allowing visiting playmates to see some part of the cat.

He dug a grave under a peach tree in his backyard, then lowered the box by a string tied around it. When the grave was filled in, part of the cat's protruding tail remained unburied. Every two or three days the boy pulled up the cat, using the tail for a handle, to investigate its condition.

How like people who confess their sins but then continue to drag them out, pull them up, spread them out, weep over them afresh, somehow forgetting that God has declared them forgiven. When Christ pardons our sins, He buries them. Let's leave them buried, and do like our Lord—remember them no more.

Joseph knew how bad their sin had been, and forgave them fully. So Christ knows the rottenness of our past, and freely forgives.

Distrust in Joseph's promise. An aviation enthusiast celebrated a man's 75th birthday by taking him for a plane ride over his hometown. Back on the ground after a half hour's flight, he asked the man if he had been scared. "No," replied the 75-year-old man, "but I never did put my full weight down!"

The brothers somehow hadn't yet put their full trust in Joseph's assertion of forgiveness. Though at first they seemed to believe Joseph's acceptance of them, they now began to doubt. So, not leaning fully on Joseph's first promise, they had to come for a second word.

Often people who claim to believe in the inspiration of the Bible do not stand on its promises. When we ask Christ's forgiveness, it's unnecessary and distrustful to go to Him again over the same sin. He cannot forgive the same sin twice, for He has already pronounced the word of forgiveness. All He can do is repeat the initial, already-given word of pardon.

That's what Joseph had to do. Reassure his brothers by reaffirming his earlier word of reconciliation.

How the Brothers' Doubts Were Dispelled

Joseph's answer to the brothers' request for mercy taught them things about Joseph which they should have found out sooner.

Their doubts saddened Joseph. "Joseph wept when they spake unto him" (50:17). He suffered surprise, shock, sorrow, and pain. After all the tangible demonstration of his love for nearly 20 years, how could they think him a wretch just waiting to take revenge? The very thought brought tears.

Likewise, the Saviour is hurt when we doubt His forgiveness. In fact, to accept His pardon and then doubt our salvation is to virtually call God a liar. These seem strong words, but are not one whit stronger than Scripture. John wrote, "This is the record, that God hath given to us eternal life, and this life is in His Son. He that hath the Son hath life; . . . he that believeth not God hath made Him a liar; because he believeth not the record that God gave of His Son" (1 John 5:10-12).

Joseph's full forgiveness. Joseph told them he was not their judge, "Am I in the place of God?" He couldn't pass judgment, but only forgive. He repeated the very same comforting explanation he had given nearly 20 years before. "Ye thought evil against me; but God meant it unto good, to bring to pass, as it is this day, to save much people alive" (50:19-20).

The Christian who doubts his salvation needs to

understand that grace is undeserved favor. Our sinful deeds deserve eternal punishment. But instead of receiving our just desert, we receive pardon and adoption into the family of God on the basis of Christ's sacrificial death on the cross. We should be sent to hell, but by grace we are destined for heaven. All of this is not because of anything we have done or could ever do, but through the loving-kindness, mercy, and love of the Lord Jesus. "Where sin abounded, grace did much more abound" (Rom. 5:20). Amazing grace!

A deacon was authorized to take $50 from a church fund to a poor lady. Though he knocked and knocked on her poor shack, she did not answer. Meeting her on the street later, he mentioned he had been there. "Oh," she sighed, "I thought it was the man calling for the rent." Christ could collect the rent and send us to hell. But He comes offering not only to pay the rent, but to give us His riches.

If years after our conversion we come to see how big our earlier sins were, then we should say, "Lord, I didn't realize the enormity of my sin. But I now see the greatness of Your grace in forgiving me such big sins."

Joseph's faithfulness to his promise. Joseph reassured his brothers. Twice he said, "Fear not" (50:19, 21). He promised to nourish them and their little ones. "And he comforted them, and spake kindly unto them" (50:21). His word, now reaching their hearts with great impact, dispelled their doubts. They rested on his promise.

Doubters need to look afresh at Christ's promises, then rest on them. His words of promise feed our faith, dismiss our fears, and give peace that passes understanding. Christ taught that the person who believes on Him has eternal life, is forgiven, saved, uncondemned, justified, a child of God, and assured of heaven (John 1:12; 3:36; 5:24; Acts 13:38; 16:31).

An elderly lady was dying. To test her depth of faith her pastor asked, "What if after all, God should let your soul be lost? What then?" Firmly she replied, "Let God do as He wills, but He would lose more than I." Pressed for an explanation, she added, "True, I would lose my soul, but God would lose His veracity, His honesty." She was right. If God should let one soul be lost who has put his trust in Christ, God would no longer be true and faithful. He would lose His honor and glory. He would cease to be God.

When Dr. J. Wilbur Chapman, internationally known evangelist of a few decades ago, was a student preparing for the ministry, he lacked assurance of salvation. He told D.L. Moody his problem. "One day I'm sure that when I die I'll be in heaven. Then another day I'm in despair for I don't know for sure I'm saved." Moody pointed to John 5:24 which promises no condemnation to the believer in Christ. "Do you believe on the Son?" Moody asked. "Yes," replied the young student. "Will you come into condemnation?" asked Moody. "That's what I don't know for sure. That's why I came to see you." When Moody again asked the same question and got the same answer, he said firmly, "See here, young man, whom are you doubting?" In a flash it dawned on the young Chapman that he was doubting none other than the Lord Himself, whose Word cannot be broken. That was the beginning of better days, for Chapman never doubted from that day forward.

Forgiveness and assurance of forgiveness are two different matters. Joseph's brothers had forgiveness for nearly 20 years, but didn't have assurance of that forgiveness till they came to trust Joseph's word fully.

An exhausted refugee couple, who claimed they had walked all the way from the Soviet Union, were found hiding one July morning in a city garbage dump in Switzerland. Police said the two were clad in rags, emaciated, and so terrified when discovered that they refused to move till given a piece of paper with a handwritten promise that they would not be sent home. They were Hungarians who had fled forced labor in a Soviet mine, walking at night away from roads, and hiding during the day, mainly near garbage dumps where they sought scraps of food. Weighing less than 110 pounds each, they had eaten their last bowl of hot soup in May when passing through Hungary. Avoiding all contacts with people, they had no idea they were in Switzerland. In reality they had been free for some weeks, but didn't know it.

Some who have fled from the wrath to come through trust in Christ do not have assurance that they are safe from that judgment. They need to rest on the faithfulness of Christ to His Word. Baptist pulpiteer C.H. Spurgeon observed that salvation is the milk, and assurance of salvation, the cream. The child of God, like Joseph's brothers, needs to have both.

In midwinter a man came to the frozen Mississippi River. Unsure how strong the ice was at this lonely spot, he gently dropped to his knees, then began inching his way across on all fours. After minutes of agonizing crawling, and not quite to the middle, he heard the sound of a motor. Suddenly a truck loomed into sight. Almost before the man knew it, the truck had passed him at 30 miles an hour, soon reaching the other shore. Rising to his feet and with full weight on the ice, the man strode confidently to the other side.

Many who profess faith in Christ go through life half wondering if they will make the shore of heaven. But if they rest on the Lord Jesus Christ, He will hold them up and not let them perish.

Like Joseph's brothers, every believer needs to rise, and with doubts dispelled, walk with full assurance in the strength of His Word until he reaches heaven.

A Coffin in Egypt
Genesis 50:22-26

The topic of death was taboo during the first half of this century. But since 1964 the number of publications dealing with death has risen from 400 to more than 4,000. Courses on death and dying are now taught at more than 1,000 U.S. colleges and nursing and high schools. Even in elementary schools, pupils visit graveyards and discuss their feelings when a pet dies. Older students hear lectures on the care of the dying, visit funeral homes to quietly observe bodies laid out in a coffin, or stop at crematories to stare at the 1,800° F. heat inside the furnace.

Familiarity with death does not annul its certainty. Whether we think of it or not, death is unavoidable. No one is exempt from its sentence.

Genesis ends with "a coffin in Egypt." When Joseph died, he was embalmed, a tedious and costly process possible only for the aristocracy. After the removal of vital organs, and after treatment with many kinds of gums, spices, oils, and rich perfumes, the body was wrapped round and round with long strips of strong linen, gummed together to make an airtight shrouding, thus preserving the body from decay for thousands of years. Today mummies dating back even to days prior to Joseph are on display in museums. No people equalled the Egyptians in the art.

The Egyptians believed that a body had to be preserved in order to be reunited with the soul, which after death went through a cycle of transmigrations involving at least 3,000 years before rejoining the body. This would not be the resurrection of the body, but the resumption of the body. A despoiled mummy could never rejoin the spirit on the day of resumption. For the body to be hanged on a tree and then eaten by birds, as was Joseph's jailmate-baker, was the ultimate tragedy. Corpses were deposited in secret, safe, secure, even elaborate places like pyramids, along with tools, food, and jewelry, so the person could resume his occupation some day.

Joseph's embalmed body was probably placed in a beautifully painted box in the family resting place in Goshen. Because Joseph had left instructions for his body to be carried along when the Israelites left for Canaan, his burial spot, likely a rock-hewn cave, would be well marked by the chief men of the tribes.

For about 200 years his body remained "in a coffin in Egypt," all the time a silent reminder of truths vital for our 20th century (Gen. 50:22-26).

A Reminder of the Fact of Death

The Bible uses many graphic metaphors to depict the brevity of life: grass that withers (Ps. 103:15), flowers that fade (1 Peter 1:24), a tale that is told (Ps. 90:9), an ancient postman speeding by on horseback, an eagle swooping on unsuspecting prey (Job 9:25-26), a shadow that declines (Ps. 102:11), smoke that evaporates (Ps. 102:3), and vapor that vanishes (James 4:14).

Every time a thinking Israelite passed Joseph's tomb, he would be reminded of the fact of death. Sometimes at Egyptian feasts a mummy was brought to the table to make the guests recall their mortality.

Every time we pass a cemetery, see a funeral procession, hear of the passing of a friend, spot the obituary column, or go to a viewing at a funeral home, the same truth hits us. We'll all end up in coffins.

Life is short. Joseph's death at age 110 made his life the shortest of the patriarchs. With life expectancy now in the 70s, our lifespan will likely be far shorter than Joseph's.

When we were young, time seemed to move so slowly. Would we ever graduate from high school, get a job, marry, start our career? But looking back, we exclaim, "How quickly time has flown!"

Joseph's coffin reminds us that death comes to VIPs, even the prime minister of Egypt. The mouth that once uttered the words of wisdom, "Seven years of plenty, then seven years of famine," was now closed, and lips still. The hands that once directed the storing and dispensing of grain were now motionless. He who had saved thousands from death by starvation could not stave off death for himself. It seems that "The paths of glory lead but to the grave."

A Reminder of God's Pledge to Give Them the Promised Land

Genesis begins, "In the beginning God," and concludes with "a coffin in Egypt." Does this mean that God's creation ends in a mummy case? Or that we must write *finis* to the story of Joseph? Not at all. Genesis is only the book of beginnings, and is followed by Exodus, Leviticus, Numbers, Deuteronomy, and Joshua, which detail the escape from Egypt, the wilderness wanderings, and the conquest of Canaan.

Joseph's faith that his descendents would return to Canaan was expressed in his final words, "I die: and God will surely visit you, and bring you out of this land unto the land which He sware to Abraham, to Isaac, and to Jacob." Then Joseph made the children of Israel swear an oath, "Ye shall carry up my bones from hence" (50:24-25). Joseph's bones would be a perennial witness of God's pledge to give the sons of Jacob the Promised Land.

Joseph had known that the time would come when their journey to the Promised Land would seem impossible. The strength of the Hyksos Dynasty, the Semitic shepherd group which had put Joseph into power, was being slowly eclipsed by an internal revolt.

Moreover, he had realized that some day a Pharaoh who "knew not Joseph" would rule and enslave the Israelites. But Joseph had also believed the day would come when God would visit Israel and lead them out of Egyptian bondage into Canaan. His request for them to carry his bones along evidenced his faith. All through years of slavery his coffin would remind his people that some day Pharaoh would let them go. The Promised Land would be theirs.

In the absence of spokesmen for God through many

generations, Joseph's bones seemed to say repeatedly, "Don't forget Canaan." When burdens were increased, forcing Israelites to make bricks without straw, Joseph's bones would point up God's faithfulness. A weary Israelite, groaning under the taskmaster's whip, would sigh, "Joseph believed we wouldn't always be here, but sooner or later we would leave for Canaan. Let's brace up a little longer." Because of Joseph's bones, they encouraged themselves in the Lord.

Also, through the years of wandering, his bones ever pointed to the Promised Land. Paradoxically, Joseph who caused the Israelites to leave Canaan for Egypt reversed himself, for by his bones he pointed the way back to Canaan.

Joseph's dying statement is his only word referred to elsewhere in the Bible. Though his life was noble, it was his "dying speech" that was singled out for special note by the Holy Spirit because of its expression of faith, and included in the great gallery of the heroes of faith. "By faith Joseph, when he died, made mention of the departing of the children of Israel; and gave commandment concerning his bones" (Heb. 11:22).

Where did Joseph get his faith? Doubtless from the Word of God taught him during his 17 years at home by his father, and perhaps by his grandfather, Isaac, whose final years meshed with Joseph's life after Jacob's flight from Laban. Can't you see little Joseph on his father's lap as Jacob repeats the promises of the land made to Abraham and to Isaac? (Gen. 13:14-17; 26:2-3) Or as Jacob relates the dream on his flight from home in which he saw a ladder reaching to heaven, on which angels were ascending and descending, with the Lord above the ladder saying, "I am the Lord God of Abraham, thy father, and the God of Isaac; the land whereon thou liest, to thee will I give it, and to thy seed"? (28:13)

With faith based on the spoken pronouncements of God that he would surely give Israel the land of Canaan, Joseph wanted his bones ready for the moment, however hurried, when the trumpet sounded, so they would be carried up to the Promised Land.

When the day finally came, the Israelites did not forget their sworn obligation to Joseph of 200 years before, even though ordered out by the panic-stricken Pharaoh. The record reads, "Moses took the bones of Joseph with him; for he had straightly sworn the children of Israel, saying, 'God will surely visit you; and ye shall carry up my bones away hence with you'" (Ex. 13:19). Till Joseph's bones were buried in Shechem by the conquering Joshua some 40 years later, those bones served as a reminder to the traveling children of Israel of Joseph's faith in their ultimate possession of Canaan.

Two centuries elapsed before Joseph's statement of faith saw fulfillment. Perhaps our faith will not be rewarded for many years, not till after our lifetime. George Mueller, widely known man of faith, declared in a sermon in his 75th year that in his 54 years as a believer he had had at least 30,000 answers to prayer the same day the requests were made. Then he was quick to add that not all his prayers were promptly answered. "Sometimes I have had to wait weeks, months, or years." Then he told how once he had to wait over 11 years. "I brought the matter about

20,000 times before God, and invariably in the fullest assurance of faith, and yet 11½ years passed before the answer was given."

Then he told of a prayer still unanswered, begun when he was about 40 years old. He had prayed for the conversion of five individuals every day without exception, whether he was sick or well, on land or on sea, and regardless of pressures of engagements. A year and a half went by before the first one was converted, another five years before the second, and still another six years before the third was won. Says Mueller, "I thanked God for the three, and went on praying for the other two. These two remain unconverted. The man to whom God in the riches of His grace has given tens of thousands of answers to prayer, in the selfsame hour on which they were offered, has been praying day by day for nearly 36 years for the conversion of these two individuals, and yet they remain unconverted; . . . But I hope in God, I pray on, and look yet for the answer. Therefore, beloved brethren and sisters, go on waiting upon God, go on praying" (Roger Steer, *Delighted in God*, Wheaton, Illinois: Harold Shaw Publishers, 1975, pp. 266-267).

Though one of the two was converted before Mueller's death, the other was not saved till six years after he died, which meant that he prayed about 54 years for that person, a prayer that wasn't answered for about 60 years.

Should not Joseph's bones give 20th-century believers encouragement to keep on praying in difficult situations such as the conversion of seemingly impossible cases, and the return of wayward children? One

Sunday school teacher keeps faith up by regularly praying through a list of all the boys and girls that have passed through his classes for the last 20 years.

Even when someone passes away without a profession of Christ, faith may still have triumphed. Without giving false hope, it should be noted that we never know what transpires in a person's mind during moments before death. An unbeliever, thrown overboard in a shipwreck and presumed dead, was found safe on a raft hours later. He testified, "I'm now a Christian. In those last moments when I thought I was going down, I turned to Christ for forgiveness. Had I not been rescued, everyone would think I had gone to a lost eternity." The genuineness of his faith was then demonstrated by a godly Christian life.

Though the Israelites in Egypt had never seen Canaan, they were encouraged through Joseph's bones to believe that their descendents would some day surely set foot in that promised territory. Similarly, we who have never seen heaven, can rest assured through faith in Christ that some day we shall reach the heavenly Canaan, a paradise without terror or tear.

Do you feel enslaved in some bondage under a cruel taskmaster, hemmed in by some crippling circumstances, from which there seems no escape, now or ever? Take courage. God's promises are many and majestic. He has promsied to be with us, never to forsake us, but to sustain us, and eventually in His own timing, to bring us out of our confinement into His glorious liberty. He will surely lead us out of our Egypt into His Canaan, likely here, certainly hereafter.